"GOMBO ZHÈBES."

LITTLE DICTIONARY OF CREOLE PROVERBS,

SELECTED FROM SIX CREOLE DIALECTS.

TRANSLATED INTO FRENCH AND INTO ENGLISH, WITH NOTES, COMPLETE INDEX
TO SUBJECTS AND SOME BRIEF REMARKS UPON THE CREOLE
IDIOMS OF LOUISIANA.

BY

LAFCADIO HEARN.

British Library Cataloguing-in-Publication Data
A catalogue record for this book is available from
the British Library

LAFCADIO HEARN

Patrick Lafcadio Hearn was born in Lefkada, Greece in 1850. He was baptized in the Greek Orthodox Church, but in his infancy, his family relocated to Dublin, Ireland, where Hearn attended the Roman Catholic Ushaw College. Neither of these religious faiths stuck, however, and when he was nineteen Hearn went to the United States, where he began to work in journalism. He gained employment as a reporter for the *Cincinnati Daily Enquirer* in 1872, and became known as an investigative yet sensational journalist.

In 1877, Hearn left Cincinnati for New Orleans, where he remained for almost a decade. His writings about the city's unique cultural life, especially its Creole population and distinctive cuisine, were published in magazines such as *Harper's Weekly* and *Scribner's Magazine*. His best-known New Orleans works are *Gombo Zhèbes, Little Dictionary of Creole Proverbs in Six Dialects* (1885), *La Cuisine Créole* (1885), and *Chita: A Memory of Last Island*, a novella first published in *Harper's Monthly* in 1888. Over the decade, Hearn became a much-loved chronicler of the city; today, more books have been written about him than any former resident of New Orleans other than Louis Armstrong.

Between 1887 and 1890, Hearn worked as a correspondent in the West Indies, before settling in Japan, a country that would provide his greatest inspiration. At a time when Japan was largely unknown to Westerners, Hearn became world-famous for his writings on the country. His book *Glimpses of Unfamiliar Japan* (1894) was hugely popular, and in 1896 he began teaching English literature at Tokyo Imperial University. Hearn penned three more books concerned with Japan and Japanese culture. Amongst the best-remembered of these are his collections of Japanese ghost stories and legends, such as *Japanese*

Fairy Tales (1898) and *Kwaidan: Stories and Studies of Strange Things* (1903). Kearn died in Tokyo, Japan in 1904, aged 54. His grave is at the Zōshigaya Cemetery in Toshima, Tokyo.

INTRODUCTION.

Any one who has ever paid a flying visit to New Orleans probably knows something about those various culinary preparations whose generic name is "Gombo"—compounded of many odds and ends, with the okra-plant, or true gombo for a basis, but also comprising occasionally "losé, zepinard, laitie," and the other vegetables sold in bunches in the French market. At all events any person who has remained in the city for a season must have become familiar with the nature of "gombo fî'é," "gombo févi," and "gombo aux herbes," or as our colored cook calls it, "gombo zhèbes—for she belongs to the older generation of Creole *cuisinières*, and speaks the patois in its primitive purity, without using a single "r." Her daughter, who has been to school, would pronounce it *gombo zhairbes*:—the modern patois is becoming more and more Frenchified, and will soon be altogether forgotten, not only throughout Louisiana, but even in the Antilles. It still, however, retains originality enough to be understood with difficulty by persons thoroughly familiar with French; and even those who know nothing of any language but English, readily recognize it by the peculiarly rapid syllabification and musical intonation. Such English-speaking residents of New Orleans seldom speak of it as "Creole": they call it *gombo*, for some mysterious reason which I have never been able to explain satisfactorily. The colored Creoles of the city have themselves begun to use the term to characterize the patois spoken by the survivors of slavery days. Turiault tells us that in the towns of Martinique, where the Creole is gradually changing into French, the *Bitacos*, or country negroes who still speak the patois nearly pure, are much ridiculed by their municipal brethren:— *Ça ou ka palé ld, chè, c'est nèg:—Ça pas Créole!* "*What you talk is 'nigger,' my dear:—that isn't Creole!*") In like manner a young Creole negro or negress of New Orleans migl·t tell an aged member of his race: "*Ça qui to parlé ça pas Créole: ça c'est gombo!*" I have sometimes heard the pure and primitive Creole also called "Congo" by colored folks of the new generation.

The literature of "gombo" has perhaps even more varieties than there are preparations of the esculents above referred to;—the patois has certainly its gombo févi, its gombo filé, its "gombo zhèbes"—both written and unwritten. A work like Marbot's "Bambous" would deserve to be classed with the pure "févi";—the treatises of Turiault, Baissac, St. Quentin, Thomas, rather resemble that fully prepared dish, in which crabs seem to struggle with fragments of many well-stewed meats, all strongly seasoned with pepper. The present essay at Creole folklore, can only be classed as "gombo zhèbes"—(*Zhèbes çé feuil-chou, cresson, laitie, betu av, losé, zepinard*);—the true okra is not the basis of our preparation;—it is a Creole dish, if you please, but a salmagundi of inferior quality.

* * *

For the collection of Louisiana proverbs in this work I am almost wholly indebted to my friend Professor William Henry, Principal of the Jefferson Academy in New Orleans; not a few of the notes, Creole quotations, and examples of the local patois were also contributed by him. The sources of the other proverbs will be found under the head of Creole

Bibliography. The translations of the proverbs into French will greatly aid in exhibiting the curious process of transformation to which the negro slave subjected the language of his masters, and will also serve to show the peculiar simplicity of Creole grammar. My French is not always elegant, or even strictly correct;—for with the above object in view it has been necessary to make the translation as literal as is possible without adopting the inter-linear system. Out of nearly five hundred proverbs I selected about three hundred and fifty only for publication—some being rejected because of their naïve indecency, others because they offered mere variations of one and the same maxim. Even after the sifting process, I was partly disappointed with the results; the proportion of true Creole proverbs —proverbs of indubitably negro invention—proved to be much smaller than I had expected. Nevertheless all which I have utilized exhibit the peculiarities of the vernacular sufficiently to justify their presence.

* * *

While some of these proverbs are witty enough to call a smile to the most serious lips, many others must, no doubt, seem vapid, enigmatic, or even meaningless. But a large majority of negro sayings depend altogether upon application for their color or their effectiveness; they possess a chameleon power of changing hue according to the manner in which they are placed. (See for examples: Prov. 161, 251, or 308.) Every saying of this kind is susceptible of numerous applications; and the art of applying one proverb to many different situations is one in which the negro has no rival—not even among the Arabs themselves, whose use of such folklore has been so admirably illustrated by Carlo Landberg.

* * *

No two authors spell the Creole in the same way; and three writers whom I have borrowed largely from—Thomas, Baissac, and Turiault—actually vary the orthography of the same word in quite an arbitrary manner. At first I thought of remodeling all my proverbs according to the phonetic system of spelling; but I soon found that this would not only disguise the Creole etymology almost beyond recognition, but would further interfere with my plan of arrangement. Finally I concluded to publish the Creole text almost precisely as I had found it, with the various spellings and peculiarities of accent-uation. The reader will find *cabrît*, for example, written in four or five different ways. Where the final *t*—never pronounced in our own patois—is fully sounded, the several authorities upon Creole grammar have indicated the fact in various fashions : one spelling it *cabrîtt*; another *cabrite*, etc.

* * *

The grammatical peculiarities and the pronunciation of the several Creole dialects are matters which could not be satisfactorily treated within the compass of a small pamphlet. Some few general rules might, indeed, be mentioned as applying to most Creole dialects. It is tolerably safe to say that in no one of the West Indian dialects was the French "*r*" pro-nounced in former days; it was either totally suppressed, as in the word "*fôce*" (*force*), or exchanged for a vowel sound, as in *bouanche* (for *branche*). The delicate and difficult French sound of *u* was changed into *ou*; the sound *en* was simplified into *ê*; the clear European *o* became a nasal *au*; and into many French words containing the sound of *am*, such as *amour*, the negro wedged the true African *n*, making the singular Creole pronunciation *lanmou*, *canmarade*, *janmain*. But the black slaves from the Ivory and Gold Coasts, from Congo or Angola, pronounced diff rently. The Eboes and Mandingoes spoke the patois with varying accentuations;—it were therefore very difficult to define rules of pronunciation applicable to the patois spoken in all parts of one island like Guadaloupe, or one colonial province like Guyana. Not so in regard to grammar. In all forms of the patois (whether the musical and peculiarly picturesque Creole of Martinique, or the more fantastic Creole of Mauritius, adulterated with Malgache and Chinese words)—the true article is either suppressed or transformed into a prefix or affix of the noun, as in *femme-la* "the woman," or *yon lagrimace*, a grimace;—there is no true gender, no true singular and plural; verbs have rarely more than six tenses—sometimes less—and the tense is not indicated by the termination of the verb; there is a remarkable paucity of auxiliaries, and in some dialects none whatever; participles are unknown, and prepositions few. A very fair knowledge of comparative Creole grammar and pronunciation may be acquired, by any one familiar with French, from the authors cited at the beginning of this volume. I would also recommend those interested in such folklore to peruse the Creole novel of Dr. Alfred Mercier—*Les Saint-Ybars*, which contains excellent examples of the Louisiana dialect; and Baissac's beautiful little stories, "Recits Créoles," rich in pictures of the old French colonial life. The foreign philological reviews and periodicals, especially those of Paris, have published quite a variety of animal fables, proverbs, stories in various Creole dialects; and among the recent contributions of French ethnologists to science will be also discovered some remarkable observations upon the actual formation of various patois—strongly resembling our own Creole—in the French African colonies.

* * *

Needless to say this collection is far from perfect;—the most I can hope for is that it may constitute the nucleus of a more exhaustive publication to appear in course of time. No one person could hope to make a really complete collection of Creole proverbs—even with all the advantages of linguistic knowledge, leisure, wealth, and travel. Only a society of folklorists might bring such an undertaking to a successful issue; but as no systematic effort is being made in this direction, I have had no hesitation in attempting—not indeed to fill a want—but to set an example. *Goule passé, difil sivré:*—let the needle but pass, the thread will follow. **L. H.**

CREOLE BIBLIOGRAPHY.

— ·o· — ˗˗

☞ The selection of Haytian proverbs in this collection was made by kindly permission of Messrs. Harper Bros., from the four articles contributed by Hon. John Bigelow, to HARPER'S MAGAZINE, 1875. The following list includes only those works consulted or quoted from in the preparation of this dictionary, and comprises but a small portion of all the curious books, essays, poems, etc., written upon, or in the Creole patois of the Antilles and of Louisiana.—L. H.

BRUYÈRE (LOYS)—"Proverbes Créoles de la Guyane Française." (In l'Almanach des Traditions Populaires, 1883. Paris: Maisonneuve et Cie.)

BAISSAC (M. C.)—"Étude sur le Patois Créole Mauricien." Nancy: Imprimerie Berger-Levrault & Cie., 1880.

MARBOT—"Les Bambous." Fables de La Fontaine travesties en Patois Créole par un Vieux Commandeur. Fort-de-France, Martinique: Librairie de Frederic Thomas, 1869. (Second Edition. Both editions of this admirable work are now unfortunately out of print.)

THOMAS (J. J.)—"The Theory and Practice of Creole Grammar." Port of Spain, Trinidad: The Chronicle Publishing Office, 1869.

TURIAULT (J.)—" Étude sur le Langage Créole de la Martinique." (Extrait du Bulletin de la Société Academique.) Brest: Lefournier, 1869.

DE ST.-QUENTIN (AUGUSTE)—Introduction à l'Histoire de Cayenne, suivie d'un Recueil de Contes, Fables, et Chansons en Créole. Notes et Commentaires par Alfred de St.-Quentin. Étude sur la Grammaire Créole par Auguste de St.-Quentin. Antibes: J. Marchand, 1872.

BIGELOW (HON. JOHN)—"The Wit and Wisdom of the Haytians." Being four articles upon the Creole Proverbs of Hayti, respectively published in the June, July, August and September numbers of HARPER'S MAGAZINE, 1875.

Little Dictionary of Creole Proverbs.

[*Most of the proverbs quoted in Martinique are current also in Guadaloupe, only 90 miles distant. All proverbs recognized in Louisiana are marked by an asterisk (*). The indications, MAURITIUS, GUYANA, MARTINIQUE, HAYTI, etc., do not necessarily imply origin ; they refer only to the dialects in which the proverbs are written, and to the works from which they are selected.*]

1. Acoma tombé toutt mounn di: C'est bois pourri. (Quand l'Acoma est tombé, tout lo monde dit: C'est du bois pourri.)
   " When the Acoma has fallen everybody says: 'It's only rotten wood.' "[1]—[*Mart.*]

2. A fòce macaque caressé yche li ka touffé li. (À force de caresser son petit le macaque l'étouffe.)
   " The monkey smothers its young one by hugging it too much."—[*Mart.*]

3. Aspère[2] iéve dans marmite avant causé. (Attendez que le lièvre soit dans la marmite avant de parler.)
   " Wait till the hare's in the pot before you talk."—Don't count your chickens before they're hatched.—[*Mauritius.*]

4. Avant bois[3] d'Inde té pòté graine, macaque té nouri yche yo. (Avant que l'arbre d'Inde portâit des graines, les macaques nourissaient leurs petits.)
   " Before the Indian tree (?) bore seed the monkeys were able to nourish their young." —[*Martinique.*]

5. Avant zabocat macaque ka nouri yche li. (Avant qu'il y eût des avocados, les macaques nourissaient leurs petits.)
   "The monkey could nourish it young, before there were any avocadoes."[4]— [*Martinique.*]

---

[1] The Acoma, says Turiault, is one of the grandest trees in the forests of the Antilles. The meaning of the proverb appears to be, that a powerful or wealthy person who meets with misfortune is at once treated with contempt by those who formerly sought his favor or affected to admire his qualities.

[2] Evidently a creolization of the Spanish *esperar.*

[3] The word bois (wood) is frequently used in Creole for the tree itself; and pié-bois ("foot of the wood ") for the trunk or stump. " Yon gouòs pié-bois plis facile déraciné qu'mauvais l'habitude" (A big stump is easier to uproot than a bad habit), is a Martinique Creole dictum, evidently borrowed from the language of the white masters. I am sorry that I do not know which of the various trees to which the name bois d'Inde has been given by the Creoles, is referred to in the proverb—whether the mango, or China-berry. No tree is generally recognized by that name in Louisiana.

[4] The Avocado was the name given by the Spanish conquistadores to the Persea gratissima, whose fruit is the " alligator pear." But M. Turiault again traces the Spanish word back to the Carib word Aouacate.

6. Azourdi casse en fin; dimain tape langouti. (Aujourd'hui bien mis; demain en langouti.)
"Well dressed to-day; only a langouti[1] tomorrow."—[*Mauritius.*]

7. Azourdi soûle bon temps, dimain pagayé. (Aujourd'hui soûl de plaisir, demain la pagaye.)
"To-day drunk with fun, to-morrow the paddle." Allusion to slavery discipline.—[*Mauritius.*]

8. Azourdi tout marmites dibout làhaut difé. (Aujourd'hui toutes les marmites sont debout sur le feu.)
"All the cooking-pots are on the fire now." One man is now as good as another:—this proverb evidently refers to the abolition of slavery.—[*Mauritius*].

9. Azourdi tout femmes alle confesse, més lhére zautes tourne léglise diàbe zétte encore pécó av zautes. (Aujourd'hui toutes les femmes vont à confesse; mais quand elles reviennent de l'église le diable leur jette encore des péchés.)
"All the women go to confession now-a-days; but they no sooner return from church, than the devil piles more sins upon them."—[*Mauritius.*]

10. Babe canmarade ou pris difé, rousé ta ou. (Quand la barbe de ton camarade brûle, arrose la tienne.)
"If you see your neighbor's beard on fire, water your own."[2]—[*Martinique.*]

11. Babiez mouche, babiez viande. (Grondez les mouches, grondez la viande.)
"Scold the flies, scold the meat."—[*Hayti.*]

12. Badnèn bien èpis macaque; main pouèngûde manyèn lakhé li. (Badinez bien avec le macaque ; mais prenez garde de ne pas manier sa queue.)
"Joke with the monkey as much as you please ; but take good care not to handle his tail."—[*Trinidad.*]

13. Baggïe qui fair ziex fair nez. (Les choses qui font [mal aux] yeux, font [mal au] nez.)
"What troubles the eyes affects the nose."[3]—[*Trinidad.*]

14. Bagasse boucoup, flangourin piti morceau. (Beaucoup de bagasse, peu d jus.)
"Much bagasse and little juice." (The bagasse is the refuse of the cane, after the sap has been extracted.)—[*Mauritius.*]

15. Baignèn iches moune; main pas lavez dêïer zoreîes yeaux. (Baignez les enfants des autres [lit : du monde] ; mais ne les lavez pas derrière les oreilles.)
"Bathe other people's children ; but don't wash behind their ears."—That is to say: Do not be servile in obsequiousness to others.—[*Trinidad*].

16. Balié nef, balié prope. (Un balai neuf, un balai propre.)
"A new broom's a clean broom."—This is a Creolization of our household phrase: "A new broom sweeps clean."—[*Mauritius.*]

---

1 The langouti was the garment worn about the loins by male slaves in Mauritius—who were wont to labor otherwise naked. In Creole both *caser* and *taper* signify "to put on," with the difference that *caser* generally refers to good clothes. In colloquial French *tapé* means "stylishly dressed," "well-rigged-out," etc.
2 "Take example by the misfortune of others." I much doubt the Creole origin of any proverb relating to the *beard*. This one. like many others in the collection, has probably been borrowed from a European source; but it furnishes a fine sample of patois. In Louisiana Creole we would say *to quenne* instead of *ta ou*. The Spanish origin of the Creole *quenne* is obvious.
3 I believe there is an omission in Thomas' version, and that the Creole ought to read :. *Baggaie qui fair mal ziex fair mal nez.*" *Baggaie* has a hundred meanings: "thing," "affair," "business," "nonsense," "stuff," etc.

17. Bardeaux¹ couvert tout. (Les bardeaux couvrent tout.)
"Shingles cover everything."—Family roofs often cover a multitude of sins.
[*Mauritius*.]

18. Bâton pas fò passé² sabe. (Le bâton n'est pas plus fort que le sabre.)
"The stick is not stronger than the sabre."—[*Martinique*].

19. Batté rendé zamós fére mal. (Les coups rendus ne font jamais de mal.)
"Blows returned never hurt."—Vengeance is sweet.—[*Mauritius*.]

20. Bef pas bousoin lakhé li yon sel fois pou chassé mouche. (Le bœuf n'a pas besoin de sa queue une fois seulement pour chasser les mouches,)
"It isn't one time only that the ox needs his tail to drive the flies away."—Ironical expression for "you will have need of me again."³—[*Martinique*.]

21. Bef pas jamain ka díe savane, "Meçi!" (Le bœuf ne dit jamais à la savane, "Merci!")
    "Ox never says 'Thank you,' to the pasture."⁴—[*Trinidad*.]

22. Béfs laquée en lére, mauvés temps napas loin. (Les bœufs ont la queue en l'air, le mauvais temps n'est pas loin.)
"When the oxen lift their tails in the air, look out for bad weather."—[*Mauritius*.

23. *Bel tignon⁵ pas fait bel négresse. (Le beau tignon ne fait pas la belle negresse.)
"It isn't the fine head-dress that makes the fine negress."- [*Louisiana*.]

24. Bénéfice ratt, c'est pou sèpent. (Le bénéfice du rat, c'est pour le serpent.)
"The rat's gains are for the serpent."—[*Martinique*.]

25. Bon bagout çappe lavie. (Bon bagou sauve la vie.)
"Good gab saves one's life."—[*Mauritius*.]

26. Bon blanc mouri; mauvais rêté. (Le bon blanc meurt; le mauvais [méchant] reste.)
"The good white man dies; the bad remains."—[*Hayti*.]

27. Bon-bouche ka gagnin chouvals à cródit. (La bonne bouche⁶ obtient des chevaux à credit.)
"Fair words buy horses on credit."—[*Trinidad*.]

¹ The sarcasm of this proverb appears to be especially levelled at the rich. In other Mauritian proverbs the house of the rich man is always spoken of as the house covered with shingles, in contradistinction to the humble slave cabins, thatched with straw.
² *Passé—lit*: "past"—therefore synonymous with "beyond." Word for word the translation would be:—"The stick is not strong beyond the sword." But the Creole generally uses "plis....passé" instead of the French plus....que ("more than"). "Victorine li plis zolie passé Alphonsine"—Victorine is more pretty than Alphonsine. The Creole *passé* is really adverbial; bearing some semblance to the old English use of the word "passing," as in "*passing* strange," "*passing* fair."
³ This proverb may be found in all the Creole dialects of the West Indies. We have in the South a proverb to the same effect in English: *Flytime will come again*, and the ox will want his tail.
⁴ A proverb current in Martinique, Louisiana, etc., with slight variations. Favors or services done through selfish policy, or compelled by necessity, do not merit acknowledgment.
⁵ The Louisiana *tiyon* or *tignon* [*tiyon* is the true Creole word] is the famously picturesque handkerchief which in old days all slave women twisted about their heads. It is yet worn by the older colored folk; and there are several styles of arranging it—*tiyon chinoise, tiyon Créole*, etc. An old New Orleans ditty is still sung, of which the refrain is:—
Madame Caba!
Tiyon vous tombé!
Madame Caba,
Tiyon vous tombé!
"Madame Caba, your tiyon's falling off!"
⁶ That is to say: *la bonne langue*;—"the good tongue gets horses on credit."

28. * Bon chien pas janmain trappé bon zo. (Jamais un bon chien n'obtient un bon os.)
    " A good dog never gets a good bone."—Creole adaptation of an old French proverb.—
    [*Martinique.*]

29. Bon coq chanté dans toutt pouleillé. (Un bon coq chante dans tout [n'importe quel]
    poulailler.)
    "A good cock crows in any henhouse."—Meaning that force of character shows
    itself under all circumstances.—[*Martinique.*]

30. Bondié baille nouè∘ett pou ça qui pas ni dent. (Le Bon Dieu donne des noisettes à
    celui qui n'a pas de dents.)
    "God gives nuts to people who have no teeth." Originally an Oriental proverb;
    adopted into Creole from the French. As we say: "A fool for luck."—[*Martinique*].

31. Bon-Guè ka baille ti zouèseau dans bois mangé, jigé si li pas ké baille chritien mangé.
    (Le Bon Dieu donne à manger aux petits oiseaux qui sont dans les bois; jugez s'il ne
    donnera pas à manger à un chrétien.)[1]
    " God gives the little birds in the wood something to eat; judge for yourself, then,
    whether he will not give a Christian something to eat."—[*Martinique.*]

32. Bon lilit, bon ménaze. (Bon lit, bon ménage.)
    "Where there's a good bed, there's good housekeeping."—[*Mauritius.*]

33. Bon piè sauvé mauvais cò. (Un bon pied sauve un mauvais corps.)
    "A good (swift) foot saves a bad (weakly) body."—Like our proverbial refrain: "He
    that fights and runs away," etc.[2]—[*Martinique.*]

34. * Bon-temps fait crapaud manqué bounda. (Le bon temps fait manquer de derrière au
    crapaud.)
    "Idleness leaves the frogs without buttocks."—[*Louisiana*].

35. * Bon-temps pas bosco. (Le bon temps n'est pas bossu.)
    " Good fortune is never hunch-backed." (Same proverb in Martinique dialect, and
    in that of Louisiana.)[3]—[*Trinidad.*]

36. Bon valett ni lakhé coupé. (Le bon valet a la queue coupée.)
    " The good servant's tail is cut off."—Reference to the condition of a dog whose tail is
    cut off : he can't wag his tail, because he has no tail to wag![4]—[*Martinique.*]

37. * Bouche li pas ni dimanche. (Sa bouche n'a pas de dimanche.)
    "His mouth never keeps Sunday"—lit: ' has no Sunday"—no day of rest.—[*Mart.*]

---

1 Such a conversation as the following may not unfrequently be heard among the old
colored folk in New Orleans :—
    —" Eh ! Marie ! to papé travaï jordi ?
    —" Moin ?—non ! "
    —" Eh, ben ! comment to fé pou vive, alors ?
    —" *Ah !....ti zozo li ka boï, li ka mangé, li pas travaï toujou !* "
[" Hey, Marie !—Ain't you going to work to-day ?" "I ?—no ! " " Well then, how do you
manage to live ? " " *Ah !....little bird drinks, little bird eats, little bird does'nt work all the
same !* "
    2 Or like the Old Country saying " Better a good run than a bad stand."
    3 In Creole *bon temps* most generally signifies "idleness," and is not always used in a
pleasant sense. Prov. 35 is susceptible of several different applications.
    4 The good servant does not fawn, does not flatter, does not affect to be pleased with
everything his master does—he may emulate the dog in constant faithfulness, not in
fawning.

38. Boucoup disic dans cannes, més domaze marmites napas nous. (Beaucoup de sucre dans les cannes, mais par malheur nous ne sommes pas les marmites.)

"Plenty of sugar in the canes; but unfortunately we are not the boilers."—Said when dishonesty is discovered in the management of affairs.—[*Mauritius.*]

39. Boudin pas tini zoreles. (Le ventre n'a pas d'oreilles.)

"The belly has no ears."—[*Trinidad.*]

40. * Bouki fait gombo, lapin mangé li. (Le bouc fait le gombo, le lapin le mange.)

"He-goat makes the gombo ; but Rabbit eats it."[1]—[*Louisiana.*]

41. Ça ou jété jòdi épis piè, ou ramassé li dimain épis lanmain. (Ce que vous rejetez aujourd'hui avec le pied, vous le ramasserez demain avec la main.)

"What you push away from you to-day with your foot, you will pick up to-morrow with your hand."[2]—[*Martinique.*]

42. Ça ou pédi nen fè ou va trouvé nen sann. (Ce que vous perdez dans le feu, vous le retrouverez dans la cendre.)

"What you lose in the fire, you will find in the ashes."—Meaning that a good deed is never lost. "Cast your bread upon the waters," etc.—[*Martinique.*]

43. * Ça qui bon pou zoie, bon pou canard. (Ce qui est bon pour l'oie, est bon pour le canard.).

"What is good for the goose is good for the duck."—*Martinique.*

44. Ça qui boudé manze boudin. (Celui qui boude mange du boudin.)

"He who sulks eats his own belly." That is to say, spites himself. The pun is untranslatable."[3]—[*Mauritius.*]

45. Ça qui dourmi napas pensé manzé. (Qui dort ne pense pas à manger.)

"When one sleeps, one doesn't think about eating."[4]—[*Mauritius.*]

46. Ça qui fine goûté larac zamés perdi son goût. (Celui qui a goûté l'arac n'en oublie jamais le goût.)

"He who has once tasted arrack never forgets the taste."—[*Mauritius.*]

47. Ça qui gagné piti mil dehors, veillé laplie. (Celui qui a un peu de mil dehors veille la pluie.)

"He who has [would raise] a little millet out of doors, watches for rain."—[*Hayti.*]

48. Ça qui gagne zoli fille gagne coudeçapeau. (Celui qui a une jolie fille reçoit des coups de chapeau.)

"He who has a pretty daughter receives plenty of salutes."—[*Mauritius.*]

49. Ça qui mangé zé pas save si bonda poule fait li mal. (Ceux qui mangent ne savent pas si le derrière de la poule lui fait mal.)

"Those who eat eggs don't know whether the chicken suffered."[5]—[*Martinique.*]

50. Ça qui ni bon piè prend douvant. (Celui qui a bon pied prend le devant.)

"He who is swift of foot takes the lead." Force of character always brings its possessor to the front.—[*Mart.*]

---

[1] This proverb is founded upon one of the many amusing Creole animal-fables, all bearing the title: *Compè Bouki épis Compè Lapin*) "Daddy Goat and Daddy Rabbit".) The rabbit always comes out victorious, as in the stories of Uncle Remus.

[2] "Waste not, want not."

[3] *Boudin* in French signifies a pudding, in Creole it also signifies the belly. Thus there is a double pun in the patois.

[4] "*Qui dort, dine,*" is an old French proverb.

[5] A little too vulgar for literal translation. Those who profit by the misfortunes of others, never concern themselves about the suffering which they take advantage of.

✠ 51. Ça qui pas bon pou sac pas bon pour maconte. (Ce qui n'est pas bon pour le sac, n'est pas pour le maconte.
"What is not fit for the bag, is not fit for the maconte."[1]—[Hayti.]

52. Ça qui prend zassocié prend maite. (Celui qui prend un associé prend (se donne) un maître.
"He who takes a partner takes a master."—[Martinique.]

53. Ça qui ti bien fére, zamés ti mal fére. (Ce qui est bien fait, n'est jamais mal fait.
"What's rightly done is never wrongly done."—That is to say : Never regret anything done for a good motive.—[Mauritius.]

54. Ça qui tine poélon qui cone so prix lagresse. (C'est celui qui tient le poélon qui connaît le prix de la grasse.)
"It's the one who holds the skillet that knows the cost of lard."—[Mauritius.]

55. Ça qui touyé son lecorps travaille pour levéres. (Celui qui tue son propre corps, travaille pour les vers.)
"He who kills his own body, works for the worms." Applicable to those who injure their health by excesses.—[Mauritius.]

56. Ça qui vlé couvé, couvé su zè yo. (Ceux qui veulent couver, qu'elles couvent leurs propres œufs.)
"Let those who want to hatch hatch their own eggs."— That is, let everybody mind his or her own business.—[Martinique.]

57. *Ça va rivé dans semaine quatte zheudis. (Cela va arriver dans la semaine de quatre jeudis.)
"That will happen in the week of four Thursdays."[2]—[Louisiana.]

58. Ça zié pas voué khè pas fè mal. (Ce que les yeux ne voient pas, ne fait pas de mal au cœur.)
"What the eyes don't see never hurts the heart.[3]—[Martinique.]

59. Cabritt⁴ boué, mouton sou. (Quand la chèvre boit, c'est le mouton qui est soûl.)
"When the goat drinks, they say the sheep is drunk."—Meaning that the innocent are made to suffer for the guilty.—[Martinique.]

60. Cabritt li ka monté roche, li descende. (Chèvre qui a monté un rocher doit en descendre.)
"The goat that climbs up the rocks must climb down again.—[Guyana.]

✠ 61. Cabritt pas connaitt goumé,⁵ mais cui li batte la charge. (La chèvre ne sait pas le battre; mais son cuir [sa peau] bat la charge.)
"The goat does not know how to fight; but his hide beats the charge."—[Hayti.]

---

[1] Waïa in Trinidad Creole. Maconte is probably from the Spanish macóna, a basket without handles. The Haytian maconte is a sort of basket made of woven grass, and used for carrying all kinds of articles. It is strapped to the shoulders.
[2] Ironically said to those who make promises which there is no reason to believe will ever be fulfilled.
[3] Ce que yex ne voit, cuer ne deut, is a French proverb of the 13th century, from which was probably derived our own saying : "What the eye doesn't see, the heart doesn't grieve after."
[4] Cabri in French signifies a kid; in Creole it signifies either a kid or a goat—more generally the latter. The word was originally spelled with a final t; and the Creoles of the Antilles have generally preserved the letter, even in pronunciation. I have purposely retained the various spellings given by various authors.
[5] Goumé, or in some dialects, goumein, is said by Turiault to be a verb of African origin—Étude sur la langage Créole, page 142. Still we have the French word gourmer, signifying to curb a horse, also, to box, to give cuffs.

62. Cabritt qui pas malin pas gras. (La chèvre qui n'est pas maligne n'est pas grasse.)
"The goat that isn't cunning never gets fat."—[*Martinique.*]

63. Cabrite qui pas malin mangé nen pié morne. (La chèvre qui n'est pas maligne, mange au pied du morne.)
"The foolish goat eats at the foot of the hill."—[*Hayti.*]

64 Canari vlô rîe chôdier. (Le canari [le pot] veut rire de la chaudière [la marmite].)
"The clay-pot wishes to laugh at the iron pot."¹—[*Trinidad.*]

65. Cancrelat sourti dans lafarine. (Le cancrelat [ravet] sort de la farine.)
"The roach has come out of the flour-barrel."—Said to women of color who whiten their faces with rice-powder.—[*Mauritius.*]

66. Canna pa ni d'leau pou li baingnein i lè trouvé pou li nagé. (Le canard n'a pas de l'eau pour se laver, et il veut trouver assez pour nager.)
"The duck hasn't enough water to wash with, and he wants enough to swim in."
—Refers to those who live beyond their means.—[*Martinique.*]

67. * Capon vive longtemps. (Le capon vit longtemps.)
"The coward lives a long time."²—[*Louisiana.*]

68. * Çaquéne senti so doulére. (Chacun sent sa douleur.)
"Everybody has his own troubles."—[*Mauritius.*]

69. Çarbon zamés va done la farine. (Le charbon jamais ne donnera de farine.)
"Coal will never make flour."—You can't wash a negro white.—[*Mauritius.*]

70. Çatte boire dilhouile enbas latabe. (Le chat boit l'huile sous la table.)
"Cat's drinking the oil under the table."—People are making fun at your expense, though you don't know it.—[*Mauritius.*]

71. Çatte noir apéle larzent.³ (Un chat noir présage [appelle] de l'argent.)
"A black cat brings money (good luck.)"—[*Mauritius.*]

72. Çatte qui éna matou fére lembarras. (La chatte qui a un matou fait ses embarras.)
"The she-cat who has a tom-cat, puts on airs."—[*Mauritius.*]

---

¹ "Pot calls the kettle black." The clay pot (*canari*) has almost disappeared from Creole kitchens in Louisiana; but the term survives in a song of which the burthen is: "*Canari cassé dans difé.*"

² The word *capon* is variously applied by Creoles as a term of reproach. It may refer rather to stinginess, hypocrisy, or untruthfulness, than to cowardice. We have in New Orleans an ancient Creole ballad of which the refrain is:

Alcée Leblanc
Mo di toi, chère,
To trop capon
Pou payé ménage!
C'est qui di çi,—
Çi que di toi chère,
Alcée Leblanc!

In this case the word evidently refers to the niggardliness of *Alcée*, who did not relish the idea of settling $500 or perhaps $1,000 of furniture upon his favorite quadroon girl. The song itself commemorates customs of slavery days. Those who took to themselves colored mistresses frequently settled much property upon them—the arrangement being usually made by the mother of the girl. Housekeeping outfits of this character, constituting a sort of dowry, ranged in value from $500 to even $2,500; and such dowries formed the foundation of many celebrated private lodging houses in New Orleans kept by colored women. The quadroon housekeepers have now almost all disappeared.

³ This is certainly of English origin.

73. Çatte qui fine bourle av difé pére lacende. (Le chat qui s'est brûlé avec le feu, a peur de'
la cendre.)
   " When a cat has been once burned by fire, it is even afraid of cinders."—[*Mauritius.*]

74. Causer cé manger zorcîes. (Causer, c'est le manger des oreilles.)
   " Conversation is the food of the ears."—[*Trinidad.*]

75. C'est bon khé crâbe qui lacause li pas tini tête. (C'est à cause de son bon cœur que le
crabe n'a pas de tête.)
   "It is because of his good heart that the crab has no head." 1—[*Martinique.*]

76. *C'est couteau qui connaite çа qui dans cœur geomon. (C'est le couteau qui sait ce qu'il
y a dans le cœur du giromon.)
   "It's the knife that knows what's in the heart of the pumpkin.".2—[*Martinique.*]

77. C'est cuiller qui allé lacail3 gamelle ; gamelle pas jamain allé lacail cuiller. (C'est la cuille
qui va à la maison de la gamelle ; jamais la gamelle ne va à la maison de la cuiller.)
   " Spoon goes to bowl's house ; bowl never goes to spoon's house."—[*Hayti.*]

78. C'est douvant tambou nion connaitt Zamba. (C'est devant le tambour qu'on reconnait
Zamba.)
   "It's before the drum one learns to know Zamba."—[*Hayti.*]

79. C'est langue crapaud4 qui ka trahî crapaud. (C'est la langue du crapaud qui le trahit.)
   "It's the frog's own tongue that betrays him."—[*Trinidad.*]

80. C'est lhé vent ka venté, moun ka ouer lapeau poule. (C'est quand le vent vente qu'on
peut voir la peau de la poule—lit.: que le monde peut voir.)
   "It's when the wind is blowing that folks can see the skin of a fowl."—True character
is revealed under adverse circumstances.—[*Trinidad.*]

81. C'est nans temps laplie béf bisoèn lakhé li. (C'est dans le temps de pluie que le bœuf a
besoin de sa queue.)
   "It's in the rainy season that the ox needs his tail.—(See Martinique proverb No. 20.)
[*Trinidad.*]

82. C'est pas toutt les-jou guiabe n'empôte you pauve nhomme. (Ce n'est pas tous les jours
qui le diable emporte un homme pauvre.)
   " It isn't every day that the devil carries off a poor man."—[*Martinique.*]

83. Cé souliers tout-sêl qui save si bas tini tous. (Ce sont les souliers seuls qui savent si les
bas ont des trous.)
   "It's only the shoes that know if the stockings have holes."—[*Trinidad.*]

---

1 Implies that excessive good nature is usually indicative of feeble reasoning-pow'r.
2 This proverb exists in five Creole dialects. In the Guyana patois it is slightly different :
Couteau cûnso connain quior iniam (le couteau seul connait le cœur de l'igname.) "It's only
the knife knows what's in the heart of the yam."
3 *Caïe* or *Caïlle*, as sometimes written, is a Creole word of Carib origin. In the cities of
the Antilles *case* is generally substituted—probably derived from the Spanish *casa*, " house."
4 In some of the West Indies the French word *crapaud* seems to have been adopted by
the Creoles to signify either a toad or a frog, as it is much more easily pronounced by Creole
lips than *grenouille*, which they make sound like "gwoonouïle." But in Louisiana there is a
word used for frog, a delightful and absolutely perfect onomatopœia : OUAOUARON (wah-
wahron).
   I think the prettiest collection of Creole onomatopœia made by any folklorist is that in
Baissac's *Étude sur le Patois Créole Mauricien*, pp. 92-95. The delightful little Creole nursery-
narrative, in which the cries of all kinds of domestic animals are imitated by patois phrases,.
deserves special attention.

84. Chaque bêtè-à-fè clairé pou nânme yo. (Chaque mouche-à-feu éclaire pour son âme.
" Every fire-fly makes light for its own soul; " that is to say, " Every one for himself."—[*Martinique.*]

85. Chatt pas là, ratt ka baill[1] bal. (Absent le chat, les rats donnent un bal.)
" When the cat's away the rats give a ball."—[*Martinique.*]

86. *Chatte brilé pair di feu. (Le chat brulé a peur du feu.)
" A burnt cat dreads the fire."—[*Louisiana.*]

✗ 87. Chien connaitt comment li fait pou manger zos. (Le chien sait comment il fait pour
manger les os.)
" The dog knows how he manages to eat bones."—[*Hayti.*]

88. Chien jamain mordó petite li jusque nen zos. (La chienne ne mord jamais ses petits
jusqu'à l'os.)
" The bitch never bites her pups to the bone."—[*Hayti.*]

89. *Chien jappé li pas mordé. (Le chien qui jappe ne mord pas.)
" The dog that yelps doesn't bite."—[*Louisiana.*]

90. Chien pas mangé chien. (Les chiens ne mangent pas les chiens.)
" Dogs do not eat dogs."—[*Louisiana.*]

91. Chien qui fé caca dans chimin li blié, mais ça qui tiré pas blié. (Le chien qui fa.t caca sur
le chemin, oublie; mais celui qui l'en ôte, n'oublie pas.)
" The dog that dungs in the road forgets all about it, but the person who has to
remove it does not forget."—[*Martinique.*]

92. Chien tini guiole fòte à cafe maitò li. (Le chien a la gueule forte dans la maison de son
maître.)
" The dog is loud-mouthed in the house of his master."—[*Martinique.*]

93. Chien tini quate patte, mais li pas capabe prend quate chimin. (Le chien a quatre pattes
mais il ne peut pas [n'est pas capable de] prendre quatre chemins.)
" The dog has four paws but is not able to go four different ways [at one time]."—
[*Martinique.*]

94. Chouval rété nen zécurie, milett nen savane. (Le cheval reste dans l'écurie, le mulet
dans la savane.)
" The horse remains in the stable, the mule in the field."[2]—[*Martinique.*]

95. *Cila qui rit vendredi va pleuré dimanche. (Celui qui rit le vendredi va pleurer le
dimanche.)
" He who laughs on Friday will cry on Sunday." There is an English proverb, " Sing
at your breakfast and you'll cry at your dinner."—[*Louisiana.*]

96. Ciramon[3] pas donne calabasse. (Le giraumon ne donne pas la calebasse.)
" The pumpkin doesn't yield the calabash."—[*Hayti.*]

---

[1] *Baïll* (to give) affords example of a quaint French verb preserved in the Creole dialect,
—*bailler.* It can be found in MOLIÈRE. Formerly a Frenchman would have said, " *Bailler sa
foi, bailler sa parole.* It is now little used in France, except in such colloquialisms as , " *Vous
me la baillez belle!* "
[2] Each one must be content with his own station. Here the mule seems to represent the
slave; the horse, the master or overseer.
[3] I give the spelling *Ciramon* as I find it in Mr. Bigelow's contributions to *Harper's Magazine*, 1875. (See BIBLIOGRAPHY.) Nevertheless I suspect the spelling is wrong. In Louisiana
Creole we say *Giromon.* The French word is *Giraumon.*

97. *Cochon conné sir qui bois l'apé frotté. (Le cochon sait bien sur quel arbre [bois] il va se frotter.)

"The hog knows well what sort of tree to rub himself against."1—[*Louisiana.*]

98. Coment to tale to natte faut to dourmi. (Comment tu étends ta natte il faut que tu te couches.)

"As you spread your mat, so must you lie."—[*Mauritius.*]

99. *Compé Torti va doucement; mais li rivé coté bite pendant Compé Chivreil apé dormi. (Compère Tortue va doucement; mais il arrive au bût pendant que Compère Chevreuil dort.

"Daddy Tortoise goes slow; but he gets to the goal while Daddy Deer is asleep."2 —[*Louisiana.*]

100. Complot plis fort passé ouanga.3 (Le complot est plus fort que l'ouanga.)

2 "Conspiracy is stronger than witchcraft."—[*Haytl.*]

101. Conseillóre napas payére. (Le donneur de conseil n'est pas le payeur.)

"The adviser is not the payer." That is to say, the one who gives advice has nothing to lose.—[*Mauritius.*]

102. Coq çanté divant la porte, doumounde vini. (Quand le coq chante devant la porte quelqu'un vient.)

"When the cock crows before the door, somebody is coming."4—[*Mauritius.*]

---

1 In most of the Creole dialects several different versions of a popular proverb are current. A friend gives me this one of proverb 97 : *Cochon-marron conn² enhaut qui bois li frotté.* ("The wild hog knows what tree to rub himself upon.") *Marron* is applied in all forms of the Creole patois to *wild* things; *zhèbes marrons* signifies "wild plants." The term, *couri-marron*, or *nèque-marron* formerly designated a runaway slave in Louisiana as it did in the Antilles. There is an old New Orleans saying :

"*Après yé tiré canon*
Nègue sans passe c'est nègue-marron."

This referred to the old custom in New Orleans of firing a cannon at eight P. M. in winter, and nine P. M. in summer, as a warning to all slaves to retire. It was a species of modern curfew-signal. Any slave found abroad after those hours, without a pass, was liable to arrest and a whipping of twenty-five lashes. *Marron*, from which the English word "Maroon" is derived, has a Spanish origin. "It is," says Skeats, "a clipt form of the Spanish *cimarron*, wild, unruly; literally, "living in the mountain-tops." *Cimarron*, from Span. *Cima*, a mountain-summit. The original term for "Maroon" was *negro-cimarrón*, as it still is in some parts of Cuba.
2 Based upon the Creole fable of *Compère Tortue* and *Comperè Chevreuil*, rather different from the primitive story of the Hare and the Tortoise.

3 Di moin si to gagnin nhomme !
Mo va fé ouanga pou li ;
Mo fé li tourné fantôme
Si to vlé mo to mari....

"Tell me if thou hast a man [a lover] : I will make a *ouanga* for him—I will change him into a a ghost if thou wilt have me for thy husband."....This word, of African origin, is applied to all things connected with the voudooism of the negroes. In the song, *Dipi mo voué, toué Adile*, from which the above lines are taken, the wooer threatens to get rid of a rival by *ouanga*—to "turn him into a ghost." The victims of voudooism are said to have gradually withered away, probably through the influence of secret poison. The word *grigri*, also of African origin, simply refers to a charm, which may be used for an innocent or innocuous purpose. Thus, in a Louisiana Creole song, we find a quadroon mother promising her daughter a charm to prevent the white lover from forsaking her ; *Pou tchombé li na fé grigri*—"We shall make a *grigri* to keep him."
4 This is also a proverb of European origin. The character of Creole folklore is very different from European folklore in the matter of superstition.

103. Coudoui pas laide, temps lafôce pas lù. (Ce n'est pas laid de courir, quand on n'a pas de force.)

"It isn't ugly to run, when one isn't strong enough to stay."—[*Trin.*]

104. Coup de langue pis mauvais piqù sèpent. (Un coup de langue est plus mauvais qu'une piqûre de serpent.

"A tongue-thrust is worse than a serpent's sting."—[*Martinique.*]

105. Coudepiéd napas empéço coudecorne. (Les coups de pied n'empêchent pas les coups de corne.

"Kicking doesn't hinder butting." There is more than one way to revenge one-self.—[*Mauritius.*]

106. Coupé son nencz, volor so figuire. (Couper son nez, c'est voler sa figure.)

"Cutting off one's nose is robbing one's face."—[*Mauritius.*]

107. * Coupé zoré milet fait pas choual. (Couper les oreilles au mulet, n'en fait pas un cheval.

"Cutting off a mule's ears won't make him a horse."1—[*Louisiana.*]

108. Couroupas dansé, zaco rié. (Le couroupas [colimaçon] danse le singe rit.)

"Monkey laughs when the snail dances."2—[*Mauritius.*]

109. Çouval napas marce av bourique. (Le cheval ne marche pas avec l'âne.

"The horse doesn't walk with the ass."—Let each keep his proper place.—[*Mauritius.*]

110. Couyenade c'est pas limonade. (Couillonade n'est pas limonade.)

"Nonsense is not sugar-water" (lemonade), says Thomas. The vulgarity of the French word partly loses its grossness in the Creole.—[*Trinidad.*]

111. Crabe pas mâché, li pas gras;—li mâche touop, et li tombé nans chôdiér. (Le crabe ne marche pas, il n'est pas gras; il marche trop, et il tombe dans la chaudière).

"The crab doesn't walk, he isn't fat; he walks too much, and falls into the pot."—[*Trinidad.*]

112. * Craché nen laire, li va tombé enhaut vou nez. (Crachez dans l'air, il vous en tombera sur le nez).

"If you spit in the air, it will fall back on your own nose."3—[*Louisiana.*]

113. Crapaud pas tini chímise, ous vlé li pôte caneçon. (Le crapaud n'a pas de chemise, et vous voulez qu'il porte caleçon).

"The frog has no shirt, and you want him to wear drawers!"—[*Trinidad.*]

114. Cresson content boire dileau. (Le cresson aime à boire l'eau).

"The water cress loves to drink water." Used interrogatively, this is equivalent to the old saw: "Does a duck like water?" "Will a duck swim?"—[*Mauritius.*]

115. Croquez maconte ou oueti4 main ou ka rivé. (Accrochez votre maconte où vous pouvez l _tteindre avec la main [lit. où vôtre main peut arriver].)

"Hang up your *maconte* where you can reach it with your hand."—[*Hayti.*]

---

1 This seems to me much wittier than our old proverb: "You can't make a silk purse out of a sow's ear."

2 Probably had its origin in a Creole con'e. Same applications as Proverbs 2'6, 2'3, 315.

3 Like our proverb about chickens coming home to roost. If you talk scandal at random, the mischief done will sooner or later recoil upon yourself. I find the same proverb in the Mauritian dialect.

4 The Martinique dialect gives both *oti* and *outi* for "où": "where." Mr. Bigelow gives the curious spelling *croquz*. The word is certainly deri ed from the French, *accrocher*. In Louisiana Creole we always say 'croch' for "hang up." I doubt the correctness of the Haytian spelling as here given: for the French word *croquer* ("to devour," "gobble up," "pilfer," etc.) has its Creole counterpart; and the soft *ch* is never, so far as I can learn, changed into the k or g sound in the patois.

116. D'abord vous guetté poux de bois mangé bouteille, croquez calabasse vous haut. (Quand vous voyez les poux-de-bois manger les bouteilles, accrochez vos calabasses [en] haut). " When you see the woodlice eating the bottles, hang your calabashes out of their reach." ¹—[*Hayti.*]

117. D'abord vous guetté poux de bois mangé can ıri, calebasse pas capabe prend pied. (Quand que vous voyez les poux-de-bois manger les marmites, les calebasses ne peuvent pas leur resister).
" When you see the wood-lice eating the pots, the calabashes can't be expected to resist." ²—[*Hayti.*]

118. Dans mariaze liciens, témoins gagne batté. (Aux noces des chiens, les témoins ont les coups.)
" At a dog's wedding it's the witnesses who get hurt."—[*Mauritius.*] .

119. Dèïèr chein, cé " chein "; douvant chein, cé " Missier Chein." (Derrière le chien, c'est " chien," mais devant le chien, c'est " Monsieur le Chien.")
" Behind the dog's back it is ' dog ;' but before the dog it is ' Mr. Dog.' "—[*Trinidad.*]

120. Dent mordé langue. (Les dents mordent la langue.)
" The teeth bite the tongue."—[*Hayti.*]

121. Dents pas ka pôté dûî. (Les dents ne portent pas le deuil.)
" Teeth do not wear mourning."—meaning that, even when unhappy, people may show their teeth in laughter or smiles.—[*Trinidad.*]

122. Dent pas khé (" Dents pas cœur "—Les dents ne sont pas le cœur).
" The teeth are not the heart." A curious proverb, referring to the exposure of the teeth by laughter."³—[*Martinique.*]

123. * Di moin qui vous laimein, ma di vous qui vous yé. (Dites moi qui vous aimez, et je vous dirai qui vous êtes.)
" Tell me whom you love, and I'll tell you who you are."—[*Louisiana.*]

124. Dileau dourmi touyé dimounde. (L'eau qui dort tue les gens.)
" The water that sleeps kills people."⁴—[*Mauritius.*]

125. Dimounde qui fére larzent, napas larzent qui fére dimounde. (Ce sont les hommes qui font l'argent, ce n'est pas l'argent qui fait les hommes.)
" It's the men who make the money ; 'tisn't the money that makes the men."— [*Mauritius.*]

126. Divant camrades capabe largué quilotte. (Devant des camarades on peut lâcher sa culotte.)
" Before friends one can even take off one's breeches."—[*Mauritius.*]

---

1 Mr. Bigelow is certainly wrong in his definition of the origin of the word which he spells *queté.* It is a Creole adoption of the French *guetter,* " to watch :" and is used by the Creoles in the sense of " observe," perceive," " see." Other authorities spell it *guêtte,* as all verbs ending in " ter" in French make their Creole termination in " té." This verb is one of many to which slightly different meanings from those belonging to the original French words, are attached by the Creoles. Thus *çappe,* from *échapper,* is used as an equivalent for *sauver.*

2 The saliva of the tropical woodlouse is said to be powerful enough to affect iron.

3 The laugh or smile that shows the teeth does not always prove that the heart is merry.

4 " Still waters run deep." The proverb is susceptible of various applications. Every-one who has sojourned in tropical, or even semi-tropical latitudes knows the deadly nature of stagnant water in the feverish summer season.

127. Divant tranzés faut boutonné canneçon. (Devant des etrangers il faut boutonner son caleçon.)
"Before strangers one must keep one's drawers buttoned.—[*Mauritius.*]

128. Dizéfs canard pli gros qui dizéfs poule. (Les œufs de cane sont plus gros que les œufs do poule.
"Ducks' eggs are bigger than hens' eggs."—Quantity is no guarantee of quality.—[*Mauritius.*]

129. Dizéfs coq, poule qui fére. (Les œufs de coq, c'est la poule qui les fait.)
"It's the hen that makes the cock's eggs."—[*Mauritius.*]

130. * Dolo toujou couri larivière. (L'eau va toujours á la rivière.)
"Water always runs to the river."—[*Louisiana.*]

131. Doucement napas empéce arrivér. (Aller doucement n'empêche pas d'arriver.
"Going gently about a thing won't prevent its being done."[1]—[*Mauritius.*]

132. Fair pou fair pas mal. (Faire pour faire n'est pas [mauvais] difficile.)
"It is not hard to do a thing for the sake of doing it."—[*Trinidad.*]

133. Faut janmain mett racounn[2] dans loge poule. (Il ne faut jamais mettre un raton dans la loge des poules.
"One must never put a 'coon into a henhouse."—[*Martinique.*]

134. Faut jamais porté déil avant défint dans cerkeil. (Il ne faut jamais porter le deuil avant que le défunt soit dans le cercueil.)
"Never wear mourning before the dead man's in his coffin."[3]—[*Louisiana.*]

135. Faut páoûoles môr pou moune pè vivre. (Il faut que les paroles meurent, afin que le monde puisse vivre.)
"Words must die that people may live."—Ironical ; this is said to those who are over-sensitive regarding what is said about them."—[*Trinidad.*]

136. Faut pas cassé so maîe avant li fine mir. (Il ne faut pas casser son maïs avant qu'il soit mûr.)
"Musn't pluck one's corn before it's ripe."—[*Mauritius.*]

137. * Faut pas marré tayau[4] avec saucisse. (Il ne faut pas attacher le chien-courant (taïant) avec des saucisses.)
"Musn't tie up the hound with a string of sausages."—[*Louisiana.*]

138. Fére éne tourou pour boucé laute. (Il fait un trou pour en boucher un autre.)
"Make one hole to stop another." "Borrow money to pay a debt."—[*Mauritius.*]

139. Gambette ous trouvé gan chemin, nen gan chemin ous va pède li. (Le gambette que vous trouvez sur le grand chemin, sur le grand chemin vous le perdrez.
"Every jack-knife found on the high-road, will be lost on the high-road."[5]—[*Hayti.*]

---

1 Literally : "Gently doesn't prevent arriving." One can reach his destination as well by walking slowly, as by making frantic haste.
2 A Creole friend assures me that in Louisiana patois, the word for coon, is *chaout*. This bears so singular a resemblance in sound to a French word of very different meaning—*chat-huant* (screech-owl) that it seems possible the negroes have in this, as in other cases, given the name of one creature to another.
3 Don't anticipate trouble: "Never bid the devil good morrow till you meet him."
4 Don't cross a bridge until you come to it."
4 Adopted from old French "*taïaut*" (tally-ho !) the cry of the huntsman to his hounds. The Creoles have thus curiously, but forcibly, named the hound itself.
5 I cannot discover the etymology of this word, according to the meaning given by Mr. Bigelow. The ordinary French signification of *gambette* is "red-shank"—*Totanus caledris.*

140. Gens bon-temps kállé dîe gouvênér bon-jou. (Les gens [qui ont du] bon-temps vont dire bon-jour au gouverneur.)
   " Folks who have nothing to do (lit. : *who have a fine time*) go to bid the Governor good-day." *Gens bon-temps ;* " fine-time folks."—[*Trinidad.*]

141. *Gens fégnants ka mandé travậï épîs bouche; main khèrs yeaux ka pouïer Bondié pou yeaux pas touver. (Les gens fainéants demandent avec leurs bouches pour du travail ; mais leurs cœurs prient le Bon Dieu [pour] qu'ils n'en trouvent point.)
   " Lazy folks ask for work with their lips: but their hearts pray God that they may not find it."—[*Trinidad.*]

142. Gens qui ka ba ous conseî gagnen chouval gouous-boudin nans lhouvênaïe, nans carêmo pas ka rider ous nouri li. (Les gens qui nous donnent conseil d'acheter un cheval à gros-ventre pendant l'hivernage, ne veulent point vous aider à le nourrir pendant le carême.)
   " Folks who advise you to buy a big-bellied horse in a rainy season (when grass is plenty),won't help you to feed him in the dry season when grass is scarce."¹—[*Trinidad.*]

143. Gouïe passé difil sivré. (Où l'aiguille passe, le fil suivra.)
   " Where the needle passes thread will follow."²—[*Mauritius.*]

144. Graisse pas tini sentiment. (La graisse n'a pas de sentiment.)
   " Fat has no feeling."³—[*Trinidad.*]

145. Haillons mié passé tout nu. (Les haillons sont mieux que de rester tout nu.)
   " Rags are better than nakedness." Half-a-loaf 's better than no bread."—[*Hayti.*]

146. Haï moune; main pas ba·yeaux pañèn pou châïer dleau. (Hais les gens; mais no lour donne pas des paniers pour charrier de l'eau.)
   " Hate people; but don't give them baskets to carry water in."—that is to say : Don't tell lies about them that no one can believe—stories that "won't hold water." —[*Trinidad.*]

147. *Jadin loin, gombo gaté. (Jardin loin, gombo gâté.)
   " When the garden is far, the gombo is spoiled."⁴—[*Martinique.*]

148. *Jamais di : Fontaine, mo va jamais boi to dolo. (Ne dis jamais—Fontaine, je ne boirai jamais de ton eau.)
   " Never say—'Spring, I will never drink your water.' "⁵—[*Louisiana.*]

149. Janmain guiabe ka dòmi. (Jamais le diable ne s'endort.)
   " The devil never sleeps.—[*Martinique.*]

---

¹ This is J. J. Thomas' translation, as given in his "Theory and Practice of Creole Grammar." *Lhouvênaïe* is a word which does not exist in our Louisiana patois. Does it come from the Spanish *llover*—" to rain "? or is it only a Creole form of the French *hivernage?* *Carême*, of course means Lent; whether the dry season in Trinidad is concomitant with the Lenten epoch, or whether the Creoles of the Island use the word to signify any season of scarcity, I am unable to decide.
² When a strong man has opened the way, feebler folks may safely follow.
³ There may be some physiological truth in this proverb as applied to the inhabitants of the Antilles, where stoutness is the exception. Generally speaking phlegmatic persons are inclined to fleshiness.
⁴ This appears to be a universal Creole proverb. If you want anything to be well done, you must look after it yourself: to absent oneself from one's business is unwise, etc.
⁵ The loftiest pride is liable to fall; and we know not how soon we may be glad to seek the aid of the most humble.

150. Janmain nous ne pas douè ladans quiou poule compté zè. (Il ne faut jamais ₁nous ne devons jamais] compter les œufs dans la derrière de la poule.)
" We should never count the eggs in the body of the hen."—(The ʿ.)creole proverb is, however, less delicate.)—[*Martinique.*]

151. Jouè epis chatt ou trappé coup d'patte. (Jouez aveo le chat, et vous attrapperez un coup de patte.)
" Play with the cat, and you'll get scratched." —[*Martinique.*]

152. *Joué épis chien ou trappé pice. (Jouez avec les chiens, vous aurez des puces.)
" Play with the dogs, and you will get fleas." ¹—[*Martinique.*]

153. *Joudui pou ous, demain pou moin. (Aujourd'hui pour vous, demain pour moi.)
"To-day for you ; to-morrow for me." ²—[*Hayti.*]

154. La oti zouèseau ka fé niche yo, c'est la yo ka couché. (Où les oiseaux font leur nids, là ils se couchent.)
" Where the birds build their nests, there they sleep."—[*Martinique.*]

155. Laboue moque lamare. (La boue se moque de la mare.)
"The mud laughs at the puddle."—Like our : " Pot calls kettle black."—[*Mauritius.*]

156. Lacase bardeaux napas guétte la case vitivére. (La maison [couverte de] bardeaux ne regarde point la case couverte de vetiver.)
" The house roofed with shingles doesn't look at the hut covered with vetiver."— [*Mauritius.*]

157. * Lagniappe c'est bitin qui bon. (Lagniappe c'est du bon butin.)
" Lagniappe is lawful booty."³—[*Louisiana.*]

158. Laguer vêti pas ka pouend viéx nègues nans cabarets. (La guerre avertie ne prend pas de vieux négres dans les cabarets.)
" Threatened war doesn't surprise old negroes in the grog-shops."⁴—[*Trinidad.*]

159. * Laguerre vertie pas tchué beaucoup soldats. (La guerre avertie ne tue pas beaucoup de soldats.)
"Threatened war doesn't kill many soldiers."—[*Louisiana.*]

160. Lakhé bef dit : Temps allé, temps vini. (La queue du bœuf dit: Le temps s'en va, le temps revient.)
" The ox's tail says: Time goes, time comes."⁵—[*Martinique.*]

161. Lalangue napas lézos. (La langue n'a pas d'os).
"The tongue has no bones." This proverb has various applications. One of the best alludes to promises or engagements made with the secret determination not to keep them.—[*Mauritius.*]

---

¹ This seems to be a universal proverb. In Louisiana we say : *Joue r o e 'lichi n, etc.
² Current also in Louisiana : *Jordi pou vou*, etc.: " Your turn to-day ; perhaps it may be mine to-morrow."
³ *Lagniappe*, a word familiar to every child in New Orleans, signifies the little present given to purchasers of groceries, provisions, fruit, or other goods sold at retail stores. Groceries, especially, seek to rival each other in the attractive qualities of their *lagniappe* ; consisting of candies, fruits, biscuits, little fancy cakes, etc. The chief purpose is to attract children. The little one sent for a pound of butter, or " a dime's worth " of sugar, never fails to ask for its *lagniappe*
⁴ Proverbs 158-9 are equivalent to our " Forewarned is forearmed."
⁵ See Proverb 22. Whether the swing of the tail suggested the idea of a *pendulum* to the deviser of this saying is doubtful. The meaning seems to me that the motion of the ox's tail indicates a change not of time, but of *weather* (*temps*).

162. * Lamisère à deux, Misère et Compagnie. (La misère à deux, c'est Misère et Compagnie.)
"Misery for two, is Misery & Co." [1]—[*Louisiana.*]

163. Lapauveté napas éne vis, més li éne bien gros coulou. (La pauvreté n'est pas une vis [un vice] ; mais c'est un bien gros clou.)
"Poverty isn't a screw; but it's a very big nail." The pun will be obvious to a French reader; but *vice* is not a true Creole word, according to Baissac."—[*Mauritius.*]

164. Lapin dit : Boué toutt, mangé toutt, pas dit toutt. (Le lapin dit : Buvez tout, mangez tout, ne dites pas tout.)
"Rabbit says: Drink everything, eat everything, but don't tell everything." [2]—[*Martinique.*]

165. Laplie tombé, couroupas va sourti. (La pluie tombe, les colimaçons vent sortir.)
"It is raining ; snails will be out presently."—[*Mauritius.*]

166. * Laplie tombé, ouaouaron chanté. (Quand la pluie va tomber, les grenouilles chantent.)
"When the rain is coming, the bull-frogs sing."—[*Louisiana.*]

167. Laquée bourique napas laquée çouval. (Une queue d'âne n'est pas une queue de cheval.)
"A donkey's tail is not a horse's tail." Can't make a silk purse out of a sow's ear.—[*Mauritius.*]

168. Larzan bon, més li trop cère. (L'argent est bon, mais il est trop cher.)
"Money's good ; but it's too dear."—[*Mauritius.*]

169. Larzan napas trouvé lipied milet. (L'argent ne se trouve pas dans le pied d'un mulet.)
"Money isn't to be found in a mule's hoof."—[*Mauritius.*]

170. Larzan napas éna famille. (L'argent n'a pas de famille.)
"Money has no blood relations."—There is no friendship in business.—[*Mauritius.*]

171. * La-tché chatte poussé avec temps. (La queue du chat pousse avec le temps.)
"The cat's tail takes time to grow."—[*Louisiana.*]

172. Lepé dit aimé ous pendant li rouge doighte ous. (La lépre dit qu'elle vous aime pendant qu'elle vous ronge les doigts.)
"The leprosy says it loves you, while it is eating your fingers."—[*Hayti.*]

173. L'hére coq çanté, li bon pour marié. (Quand le coq chante, il est bon à marier.)
"When the cock begins to crow, he is old enough to get married."—[*Mauritius.*]

174. Lhére lamontagne bourlé, tout dimounde coné; lhére léquére bourlé, qui coné? (Quand la montagne brûle, tout le monde le sait; quand le cœur brûle qui le sait?)
"When the mountain burns, everybody knows it ; when the heart burns, who knows it?"—[*Mauritius.*]

175. Li allé l'ecole cabritt, li ritouné mouton. (Il est allé à l'école [comme un] cabri; il est revenu mouton.)
"He went to school a kid, and came back a sheep."[3]—[*Martinique.*]

---

[1] Refers especially to a man who marries without having made proper provision for the future. The Creole does not believe in our reckless proverb: "What will keep one, will keep two." *Non, non, chèr, lamisère d deux, Misère & Cie.!*
[2] Founded upon a celebrated Creole fable : see Prov. 40 (*note*).
[3] The allusion to the overgrown and shy schoolboy, who has lost the mischievous playfulness of his childhood, is easily recognizable. Creole planters of the Antilles generally sent their sons to Europe to be educated.

LITTLE DICTIONARY OF CREOLE PROVERBS.   23

176. Li fine vendé so coçon. (Il a vendu son cochon.)
" He has sold his pig."¹—[*Mauritius.*]

177. Li laçasse zozos pariaca. (Il chasse aux oiseaux à paliaca.)
" He's hunting paliaca-birds."²—[*Mauritius.*]

178. Li manque lagale pour gratté. (Il [ne] manque [que] de gale pour se gratter. [Lit. In good French : Il ne lui manque que la gale, etc.])
" He only wants the itch so that he may scratch himself."   Said of a man who has all that his heart can wish for.³—[*Mauritius.*]

179. Li pour marié ; més quiquefois bague mariaze glisse dans lódoight. (Il doit se marier ; mais quelquefois la bague de mariage glisse du doigt.)
" He is to be married, they say ; but sometimes the marriage-ring slips from one's finger."⁴—[*Mauritius.*]

180. Li soule bontemps. (Il se soûle de bon temps.)
" He is drunk with doing nothing."—[*Mauritius.*]

181. Liane yame ka marré yame. (La liane du yam lie [lit. amarre] le yam.)
" The yam-vine ties the yam.⁵—[*Trinidad.*]

182. Lilit pour dé napas lilet pour trois. (Un lit pour deux n'est pas un lit pour trois.)
" A bed for two isn't a bed for three.—[*Mauritius.*]

183. Lizié napas óna balizaze. (Les yeux n'ont pas de frontière.)⁶
" Eyes have no boundary."   Equivalent to the English saying : " A cat may look at a king."—[*Mauritius.*]

184. Macaque caresser iche li touop, li fourrer doègt nans ziex li. (Le macaque, en caressant trop son petit, lui a fourré le doigt dans l'œil.)
" By petting her young one too much, the monkey ends by poking her finger into its eye."—[*Trinidad.*]

185. * Macaque dan calebasse. (Le macaque dans la calebasse.)
" Monkey in the calabash."⁷—[*Louisiana.*]

186 * Macaque dit si so croupion plimé ças pas gâdó lezautt. (Le macaque dit que si son croupion est plumé, ça ne régarde pas les autres.)
" Monkey says if his rump is bare, it's nobody's business.⁸—[*Louisiana.*]

¹ Said of one who unexpectedly disburses a considerable sum, or who spends more money than his visible resources admit of.
² *Paliaca* is the Mauritian term for the brightly-colored kerchief there worn by all young negresses in lieu of hats or bonnets, like the old time Louisiana *tiyon*. " He is hunting for paliaca-birds " therefore means, " He is running after the colored girls."
³ We have a singular expression in Louisiana : " *Li metté mantec dans so faillots.* (He puts lard in his beans.") That is to say, "He is well off." *Mantec* is a Creolised form of the Spanish *mantecc*, used in Spanish-America to signify lard.
⁴ " There's many a slip twixt the cup and the lip."
⁵ In Martinique Creole the proverb is: *Còde gnâme marré gnâme.* " Còde " (*corde*) signifying the same as *llane*, the long cord-like stalk of the creeper. Folks are sometimes caught fast in the snares they set for others, just as the yam is tied with its own stalk.
⁶ The Mauritian Creoles have adopted a marine word in lieu of the French term *frontière*. " Balizaze " is the Creole form of the French *balisage*, from *balise*, a sea mark, buoy—word adopted in our own nautical technology. The term completely changes its meaning as well as its spelling in Creole.
⁷ Allusion to the old fable about the monkey, who after putting his hand easily into the orifice of a gourd, could not withdraw it without letting go what he sought to steal from within, and so got caught. In the figurative Creole speech one who allows his passions to ruin or disgrace him, is a *macaque dans calebasse.*
⁸ Allusion to the callosities of the monkey. Plimé literally means "plucked ;" but the Creole negroes use it to signify "bare" from any cause. A negro in rags might use the above proverb as a hint to those who wish to joke him about his personal appearance.

187. * Macaque pas jamain ka dîe îche li laide. (Le macaque ne dit jamais que son petit est laid.)
"Monkey never says its young is ugly."[1]—[*Trinidad.*]

188. Macaque save qui bois li monté; li pas monté zaurangé. (Le macaque sait sur quel arbre il doit monter; il ne monte pas sur l'oranger.)
"The monkey well knows what tree to climb; he doesn't climb an orange tree."[2]—[*Martinique.*]

189. Magré sèpent ni ti ziè li ka vouè clè bien. (Bien que le serpent ait de petits yeux, il voit très-clair.)
"Though the serpent has little eyes, he sees very well."—[*Martinique.*]

190. Maite cabrite mandé li; ous pas capabe di li plainda. (Le maître du cabrit le demande, vous ne pouvez pas vous en plaindre.)
"The kid's owner asks for it; you can't blame him."[3]—[*Hayti.*]

191. Maladie vine lâhaut iéve; li alle lâhaut tourtie. (La maladie vient sur le lièvre ; elle part [s'en va] sur la tortue.)
"Sickness comes riding upon a hare; but goes away riding upon a tortoise."—[*Mauritius.*]

192. Mal hé pas ka châger con lapliè. (Lit: Le malheur ne se charge pas comme la pluie.)
"Misfortune doesn't threaten like rain."[4]—[*Trinidad.*]

193. Mamans ka fair iches, main pas khèrs yeaux. (Les mères font les enfants, mais non pas leurs cœurs.)
"Mothers make children ; but not children's hearts."—[*Trinidad.*]

194. Manger yon fois pas ka rìser dents. (Manger une fois n'use pas les dents.)
"Eating once doesn't wear out the teeth."—[*Trinidad.*]

195. Mari napas trouvé dans vétivére. (Un mari ne se trouve pas dans le vétiver.)
"You won't find a husband in the *vetiver.*"[5]—[*Mauritius.*]

196. Mariaze napas pariaze; ménaze napas badinaze. (Le mariage n'est pas un pari ; le ménage n'est pas un badinage.)
"Marriage is no trifling wager, and housekeeping is no sport."—[*Mauritius.*]

197. Marié éne boutéye vide. (Epouser une bouteille vide.)
"Marry an empty bottle."—Meaning to marry a girl without a dowry.—[*Mauritius.*]

198. * Maringouin perdi so temps quand li piquó caïman. (Le maringoin perd son temps quand il pique le caïman.)
"The mosquito loses his time when he tries to sting the alligator."[6]—[*Louisiana.*]

---

[1] A widely-spread proverb. In Louisiana we say *pìti li* or *so pìti* instead of "yche" or "iche li." In Martinique Créole: *Macaque pas jamnain trouce yche li laide.*
[2] Because the orange tree is thorny.
[3] Mr. Bigelow, in *Harper's Magazine*, explains the use of this proverb by a creditor to a debtor.
[4] *Le temps se charge*, in French signifies that it is clouding up, threatening rain—lit: "loading up." Misfortune does not th eaten before it falls.
[5] The delightfully fragrant grass, well-known to pharmaceutists as the *Andropogon muricatus* or *Vetiveria odorata* is used in Mauritius to thatch cabins with. A broad border of this grass is usually planted around each square of sugar-cane. It grows tall enough to conceal a man, or a couple of lovers holding a rendezvous. Hence the wholesome warning.
[6] Ripost to a threat—as we would say: "All that has as little effect on me as water on a duck's back!"

199. Marré conm yon paqué crabe. (Amarré comme un paquet de crabes.)
"Tangled up, or tied up, like a bundle of crabs."—Said of people notoriously clumsy.[1]
—[*Martinique.*]

200. Mégue coment çatte qui manze lérats-misqué. (Maigre comme un chat qui mange des rats musqués.)
"Thin as a cat that lives on musk-rats."—[*Mauritius.*]

201. Même baton qui batte chein nouèr-là, pó batte chein blanc-là. (Le même bâton qui bat le chien noir peut battre le chien blanc.)
"The same stick that beats the black dog can beat the white."[2]—[*Trinidad.*]

202. Menti ça pas si mal conm palé mal moun. (Le mensonge n'est pas si mauvais que de parler mal des autres.)
"Lying isn't as bad as speaking badly about people."—Lying is less wicked than calumny.—[*Martinique.*]

203. * Merci pas couté arien. (" Merci " ne coûte rien.)
"Thanks cost nothing."—[*Louisiana.*]

204. * Metté milâte enhaut choual, li va dî négresse pas so maman. (Mettez un mulâtre [en haut] sur un cheval—il [va dire] dira qu'une négresse n'est pas sa maman.)
"Just put a mulatto on horseback, and he'll tell you his mother was'nt a negress."[3]—[*Louisiana.*]

205. Mié vaut mangé lamori ou, qu'codeinne leszautt. (Il vaut mieux de manger [de] la morue [qui est] à vous que le coq-d'Inde aux autres.)
"Better to eat one's own codfish than another person's turkey-cock."—[*Martinique.*]

206. Milatt ka batt, cabritt ka mò. (Les mulâtres se battent, ce sont les cabrits qui meurent.)
"When the mulattoes get to fighting, the goats get killed."[1]—[*Martinique.*]

207. Misè fè macaque mangó piment. (La misère force le macaque à manger du piment.)
"Misery makes the monkey eat red pepper."—[*Martinique.*]

208. * " Mo bien comm mo yé," parole rare. (" Je me trouve bien comme je suis"—ces sont des paroles rares.)
" ' I'm well enough as I am,' are words one doesn't often hear."—[*Louisiana.*]

209. * Mo va pas prêté vous bâton pou cassé mo latête. (Je ne vais vous prêter un bâton pour me casser la tête.)
"I'm not going to lend you a stick to break my head with."—[*Louisiana.*]

---

1 Anyone who has ever seen a heap of live crabs in a basket, will comprehend the fun of this saying—intimating that the sinews of the gawkish person are tangled up as hopelessly as crabs in a market-basket.
2 As one should observe: "I've whipped better men than you."
3 I usually give but one example of a proverb when it occurs in several dialects; but the Martinique form of this proverb is too amusing to omit. See Prov. 267.
4 The feeling of the black to the mulatto is likewise revealed in the following dicton:—
Nègue pôté maïs dans so lapoche pou volé poule ;—milatt pôtó cordon dans so lapoche pou volé choual ;—nhomme blanc pôté larzan dans so lapoche pou trompé fille. (Le négre porte du maïs dans sa poche pour voler des poules ;—le mulâtre porte un cordon dans sa poche pour voler des chevaux ;—l'homme blanc porte de l'argent dans sa poche pour tromper les filles.)
"The negro carries corn in his pocket to [help him to] steal chickens ; the mulatto carries a rope in his pocket to steal horses; the white man carries money in his pocket to deceive girls."—[*Louisiana.*]

210. Moin ainmein plis yon balaou jôdi là qu'taza dimain. (J'aime mieux un balaou aujourd'hui qu'un tazard demain.)
"I'd rather have horn-fish to-day, than mackerel to-morrow."[1]—[*Martinique.*]

211. Moin pas ka prend dithé pou flève li. (Je ne veux pas prendre du thé pour sa flèvre.)
"I don't propose to drink tea for his fever."[2]—[*Martinique.*]

212. Montagnes zamés zoinde, domounde zoinde. (Les montagnes ne se rencontrent jamais, les hommes se rencontrent.)
"Mountains, only, never meet; men meet."—We are certain to encounter friends and enemies under the most unlikely circumstances."—[*Mauritius.*]

213. Mounn ouè défaut les-zautt, yo pas ni zié pou ta yo. (Les gens voient les défauts des autres, ils n'ont pas d'yeux pour les leurs.)
"Folks see the faults of others; they have no eyes for their own "[3]—[*Martinique.*]

214. Moustique pitit; més lhére li çanté vous zoréye plein. (Le moustique est petit; mais quand il chante, votre oreille en est pleine.
"The mosquito is little; but when he sings, your ears are full of him."—[*Mauritius.*]

215. Napas éna fromaze qui napas trouve so macathia. (Il n'y a pas de fromage qui ne trouve son pain bis.)
"There's no cheese but what can find brown bread."[4]—[*Mauritius.*]

216. Napas rémié fimié sec. (Ne remuez pas le fumier sec.)
"Don't stir up dry manure."—Said to those who desire to resurrect forgotten scandal.—[*Mauritius.*]

217. Napas vous sangsie qui a monté làhaut moi. (Ce n'est pas votre sangsue qui montera sur moi.)
"Your leech isn't going to climb on me." That is: you shan't take advantage of me.
—[*Mauritius.*]

218. Napas vous laliane darzent qui a monté làhaut mo tonelle. (Ce n'est pas votre liane d'argent qui montera sur ma tonnelle.)
"It isn't your silver creeper that is going to climb over my summer house."[5]—
[*Mauritius.*]

---

[1] "A bird in the hand is worth two in the bush." The translation is not literal. The *tazard* or *thazard*, although belonging to the scomber family, is not a true mackerel. *Balaou* is one Creole name for *l'aiguillette de mer*, hornfish [?].

[2] Or better still: I don't intend to drink tea just because he has the fever." In other words, "I don't intend to bother myself with other people's troubles."....The tea referred to is one of those old Creole preparations taken during fevers—the *tisânes* of the black nurses: perhaps the cooling sassafras, or orange-leaf tea administered to sufferers from *dengue* in New Orleans.

[3] This proverb, not being of true Creole origin, receives a place here as an illustration of effective patois. In Louisiana we never say *tâ yo*, but *so quenne*....Were all proverbs used by the Creole-speaking people included in this collection, it would be considerably longer. Nearly all familiar English proverbs have received Creole adoption, with slight modifications; for example, instead of "putting the cart before the horse," the Mauritian negro *mette çarette divant milét*, puts the cart before the *mule*—an animal with which he is more familiar.

[4] That is to say, whoever has a bit of cheese can always find a bit of brown bread to eat with it. There never was a girl so ugly that she could not find a husband.

[5] Said by young girls to those whose advances are disagreeable. *Khè lanmou pas ka sauté* ("heart-of-love does not yet leap") would be the more polite response of a Martinique girl.

219. *Napas zoué av difé; wou a boulé vous çimise. (Ne jouez pas avec le feu; vous vous brûlerez la chemise.)
"Play with the fire and you'll burn your shirt." This proverb appears to be current wherever any form of the patois prevails."—[*Mauritius*,]

220. Nîon doight pas jamain mangé calalou. (Avec un seul doigt on ne peut jamais manger du calalou.)
"You can't eat calalou with one finger."[1]—[*Hayti*.]

221. Nhomme mort, zhèbes ka lever douvant lapôte li. ([Quand] un homme [est] morte, l'herbe pousse [lit. : s'élève] devant sa porte.)
"When a man is dead, the grass grows tall before his door."—[*Trinidad*.]

222. Nououi chouval pou baille zofficié monté. (Nourir des chevaux pour les donner à monter aux officiers.)
"Feed horses for officers to ride." To be the victim of one's own foolish liberality."
—[*Martinique*.]

223. *Oîmso soulié savé si bas tini trou. (Le soulier seul sait si le bas a un trou.)
"The shoe only knows whether the stockings have holes."[2]—[*Guyane*.]

224. Oti tini zos tini chien. (Où il y a des os il y a des chiens.)
"Wherever there are bones, there are dogs." Meaning that when one is rich, one has plenty of friends."—[*Martinique*.]

225. Ou faché avec gan chemin, que côté ou va passé? (Vous vous fachez avec le grand chemin, de quel côté irez-vouz?)
"If you get angry with the high road, what way will you go?"—[*Hayti*.]

226. Ou fait semblant mourir, moin fait semblant enterrer ou. (Faites semblant de mourir, et moi je ferai semblant de vous enterrer.)
"You pretend to die; and I'll pretend to bury you." [3]—[*Hayti*.]

227. Ou sauté, ou tombé la menme. (Vous sautez, vouz tombez tout de même.)
"You jump, but you come down all the same."[4]—[*Martinique*.]

228. *Où y'en a charogne, y'en a carencro. (Où il a charogne, il y a des busards.)
"Wherever there's carrion, there are buzzards." [5]—[*Louisiana*.]

229. Ous pôncor travesser lâivïèr;—pas jirez maman caïman. (Vous n'avez pas encore traversé la rivière—ne jurez [maudissez] pas la maman du caïman.)
"You haven't crossed the river yet; don't curse at the crocodile's mother."[6]—[*Trinidad*.]

---

[1] The West Indian *calalou* is made almost precisely like our *gombo*-soup. The word is of African origin according to Turiault.
[2] In the Martinique dialect it is: *C'est sou'lié qui save si bas tini trou.* In the Trinidad patois: *Cé soulier tout-sêl qui save si bas tini trou* (Thomas). In Louisiana Creole: *Cést soulier nek connin si bas gagnin trou.* "Nek," compound from French *ne ... que*—"only."
[3] Said to those who relate improbable stories of woe."
[4] Just so high as' you jump, so great the fall. The higher our ambition, the greater the peril of failure.
[5] This is one of several instances of the Creole adoption of English words. The name "carrion-crow" has been applied to the buzzard in Louisiana from an early period of its American history.
[6] "Don't halloo till you're out of the wood!"

230. Padon pas ka guéri bosse. (" Pardon " ne guérit pas la bosse.)
"Asking pardon doesn't cure the bump." 1—[*Martinique.*]

231. Pâlér pas rimède. (Parler n'est pas un reméde.)
"Talking is no remedy." In Creole the word signifies medicine as well as *remedy.*
—[*Trinidad.*]

232. Pâler touop ka lever chein nans dômi. (Trop parler [c'est çe qui] éveille le chien en dormi.)
"Talking too much arouses the dog from sleep." 2—[*Trinidad.*]

233. Pâoûoles pas tini coulèr. (Les paroles n'ont pas de couleur.)
" Words have no color."—This is generally said to people who stare a speaker out of countenance.—[*Trinidad.*]

234. Pâoûoles pas couté cher. (Les paroles ne coûtent pas cher.)
"Words are cheap." In Martinique the phrase is *Paoûôles pas châge:* (" Words are no weight to carry.")—[*Trinidad.*]

235. *Parole trop fort, machoir gonflé. (Par la parole trop forte, la machoir est gonflée.)
" By talking too loud the jaw becomes swelled." 3—[*Louisiana.*]

236. Pas fôte langue qui fair bef pas sa pâler. (Ce n'est pas à faute de langue que le bœuf ne sait pas parler.)
"It isn't for want of tongue that the ox can't talk."—[*Trinidad.*]

237. Pas jou' moin bien changé, moin ka rencontré nénneine moins. (Ce n'est pas le jour que je suis bien changé que je vais rencontrer ma marraine.)
"It isn't on the day I am greatly changed" [when I am most unfortunate] "that I am going to meet my godmother."—[*Martinique.*]

238. Pas menme jou ou mangé tè ou vini enflé. (Ce n'est pas le même jour que vous mangez que vous vous trouvez enflé).
"It isn't the same day you eat that you find yourself puffed up." 4—[*Martinique.*]

239. Pauve moune bail déjeuner nans quior. (Les pauvres gens vous donnent à déjeuner dans leurs cœurs).
"Poor folks give breakfast with their hearts."—[*Hayti.*]

240. * Pis faibe toujou tini tô. (Le plus faible a toujours tort).
" The weakest is always in the wrong."—[*Martinique.*]

241. * Fiti à piti, zozo fait son nid. (Petit à petit, l'oiseau fait son nid.)
" Little by little the bird builds its nest."— [*Louisiana.*]

---

242. Piti pas coûté so moman, li ka mori gran solé midi. (Petit qui n'écoute pas sa maman meurt au grand soleil de midi).

"Little boy who won't listen to his mother dies under the noonday sun." [1] [*Guyana.*]

243. Plis vaut mié vous pitit gagne larhime qui vous arrace son nez. (Il vaut mieux laisser votre enfant morveux que de lui arracher le nez).

"Better let your child be snotty, than pull his nose off."—[*Mauritius.*]

244. Pou manje. tou bon; pou pâlé pas tou parole. (Pour manger, tout est bon ; pour parler, pas toute parole).

"Anything is good enough to eat; but every word is not good enough to be spoken." [2] —[*Guyane.*]

245. Poule pas ka vanté bouillon yo. (Los poules ne vantent pas leur [propre] bouillon.)

"The chickens don't brag about their own soup;" i. e. *chicken-soup.*—[*Martinique.*]

246. Poule qui çanté ça mémé qui fine pondé. (La poule qui chante est celle-là même qui a pondu).

"It's the cackling hen that has laid the egg."—[*Mauritius.*]

247. Poule qui fére dè dizèfs zamés touyé. (La poule qui fait deux œufs n'est jamais tuée).

"The hen that lays two eggs is never killed."—[*Mauritius.*]

248. * Pranne garde vaut miè passé mandé pardon. (Prendre garde vaut mieux que demandre pardon.)

"It is better to take care beforehand than to ask pardon afterward."—[*Louisiana.*]

249. Ptit lasoif ptit coco, grand lasoif grand coco. (Petite soif, petit coco ; grande soif, grand coco.)

"Little thirst, a little cocoa-nut; big thirst, a big cocoa-nut." [4]—[*Mauritius.*]

250. Ptit mie tombe, ramassé li ; Chrétien tombe, pas ramassé li. (Quand une petite mie tombe, on la ramasse ; quand un Chrétien tombe, on ne le ramasse pas [i. e., on ne l'aide pas à se relever].)

"If a little crumb falls, it is picked up ; if a Christian falls, he is not picked up."— [*Hayti.*]

251. * Quand bois tombé, cabri monté. (Quand l'arbre tombe, le cabri monte.)

"When the tree falls, the kid can climb it."—[5][*Louisiana.*]

252. Quand boudin mòdè, cé pas épi bell plimmé yo ka pleiu li. (Quand le ventre crie, ce n'est pas avec de beaux habits qu'on le remplit.)

"When your stomach gnaws you, it isn't with fine clothes that you can fill it."— [*Martinique.*]

1 All Creole mothers are careful to keep their children from reckless play in the sun, which is peculiarly treacherous in those latitudes where the dialect is spoken. Hence the proverb, applicable to any circumstance in which good advice is reluctantly received.
2 In the Martinique dialect: *Toutt mangé, toutt paaule pas bon pou di.*--[*Turiault.*]
3 The sound of the French *eu* is rarely preserved in Creole. *L heure* becomes *lhère ; peu,* becomes *pé.* The Creole-speaking negro says, *Yonne, dè, tois, quate, nèf,* instead of "un, deux, trois, quatre, neuf."
4 Like the old-country saying : "Big horse, big feed." The cocoa-nut shell was formerly the slave's drinking cup in Mauritius.
5 This saying has quite a variety of curious applications. The last time I heard it, a Creole negress was informing me that the master of the house in which she worked was lying at the point of death: "*pauve diabe!*" I asked after the health of her mistress. "*Ah! Madame se porte bien ; mais . . . quand bois tombé cabri monté,*" she replied, half in French, half in her own patois ; signifying that after the husband's death, wife and children would find themselves reduced to destitution.
6 Literally "feathers"—"*plimm,*" *plumes.* Adopted from a Creole version of one of Lafontaine's fables.

30   LITTLE DICTIONARY OF CREOLE PROVERBS.

253. *Quand boyaux grogné, bel 'evite pas fait yé pé. (Quand les boyaux grognent, un bel
    habit ne leur fait pas se taire ; lit., ne leur fait pas paix.)
    " When the bowels growl a fine coat won't make them hold their peace."¹—[*Louisiana.*]

254. Quand cannari pas bouï pou ou, ou donè janmain découvri li. (Quand le pôt ne bout
    pas pour vous, vous ne devez jamais le découvrir.)
    " When the pot won't boil for you, you must never take the lid off." ²—[*Martinique.*]

255. Quand canon causé, fisil honté. (Quand le canon parle, le fusil a honte.)
    " When the cannon speaks, the gun is ashamed."—[*Mauritius.*]

256. Quand diabe alle lamesse li caciétte so laquée. (Quand le diable va à la messe, il cache
    sa queue.)
    " When the Devil goes to mass he hides his tail."—[*Mauritius.*]

257. Quand diabe voulé prend vous li cause bondié av vous. (Quand le diable veut vous
    prendre il vous parle de Bon Dieu.)
    " When the devil wants to get hold of you, he chats to you about God." Lit.: " He
    talks *Good God* to you."—[*Mauritius.*]

258. Quand done vous bourique vous pas bisoin guétte so labride. (Quand on vous donne un
    âne, vous ne devez pas regarder sa bride.)
    " When somebody gives you a donkey, you musn't examine the bridle."—Never look
    a gift-horse in the mouth.—[*Mauritius.*]

259. Quand femme léve so robe diabe guétte so lazambe. (Quand une femme relève sa robe
    le diable regarde sa jambe.)
    " When a woman lifts her dress, the devil looks at her leg."—[*Mauritius.*]

260. Quand gagne larmoire napas quétte côffe. (Quand on a l'armoire on ne regarde pas les
    coffre.)
    "As soon as one gets a clothes-press, one never looks at the trunk."³—[*Mauritius.*]

---

¹ The words *pè*, *pé*, in Creole are distinguishable only by their accentuation. *Peur* (fear) ;
peu (a little) ; *paix* (peace, or " hush ") ; *peut* (can), all take the form *pè* or *pé* in various Creole
dialects. *Ipas ni pè sépent ;* "he is not afraid of snakes." Sometimes one can guess the
meaning only by the context, as in the Martinique saying: *Pè bef pè caca bef.* "Few oxen,
little ox-dung ;" i. e., "little money, little trouble." The use of "*pè*" for *père* (father),
reminds us of a curious note in the Creole studies of the brothers Saint-Quentin (See BIBLIO-
GRAPHY). In the forests of Guiana there is a bird whose song much resembles that of our
Louisiana mocking-bird, but which is far more sonorous and solemn. The Creole negroes
call it ZOZO MONPÉ (*l'oiseau mon-père*), lit., "The my-father bird." Now *monpè* is the Creole
name for a priest; as if we should say " a my-father "instead of " a priest." The bird's song,
powerful, solemn, far-echoing through the great aisles of the woods by night, suggested the
chant of a *monpè*, a "ghostly father;" and its name might be freely translated by " the
priest-bird."
² " Watched pot never boils." The *canari* was a clay pot as the following Creole refrain
testifies :
              Ya pas bouillon pou vous, macommère ;
              Canari cassé dans difé (bis),
              Bouillon renvèrsé dans difé
              Ya pas bouillon pou vous, macommère
              Canari cassé dans difé.
[" There's no soup for you, my gossipping friend ; the pot's broken in the fire; the soup is
spilled in the fire," etc.]
³ A wooden chest or trunk is the first desideratum of the negro housewife. As soon
as the family is able to purchase a clothes-press, or (as we call it in Louisiana) " armoire,"
it is considered quite a prosperous household by Mauritian colored folk. The chest,
Baissac tells us, is the clothes-press of the poor. "After the bed comes the chest, and next
the accordeon !"

261. Quand lamôrt vini, vous pense vous lavie. (Quand la mort vient, vous pensez à vôtre vie.)
" It's when death comes that you think about your life."—[*Mauritius.*]

262. Quand lébras trop courte, napas zoindo. (Quand les bras son trop courts, ils ne se rejoignent pas.)
" When one's arms are too short, they won't go round."1—[*Mauritius.*]

263. Quand lécie tombé, tout mouces va maillé. (Quand le ciel tombera, toutes les mouches seront prises.)
" When the sky falls all the flies will be caught."2—[*Mauritius.*]

264. * Quand li gagnin kichose dans so latête, cé pas dans so lapiè. (Quand il a quelque chose dans sa tête, ce n'est pas dans son pied.)
" When he gets something into his head, it isn't in his foot."3—[*Louisiana.*]

265. Quand lipièd glissé, restant sivré. (Quand le pied glisse, le reste suit.)
" When the foot slips the rest follows."—[*Mauritius.*]

266. Quand maite chanté, nègue dansé ; quand 'conomə sifflé, nègue sauté. (Quand le maître chante, le nègre danse; quand l'économe siffle, le nègre saute.)
" When the master sings the negro dances; but when the overseer only whistles, the negro jumps."—A relic of the old slave-day Creole folklore.—[*Louisiana.*]

267. Quand milatt tini yon vié chouvral yo dit nègress pas manman yo. (Quand les mulâtres ont un vieux cheval ils disent que les négresses ne sont pas leurs mères.)
" As soon as a mulatto is able to own an old horse, he will tell you that his mother wasn't a nigger." [*Martinique.*]

268. * Quand napas maman, tété grand-maman. (Quand n'a pas sa mère, on tete sa grand-mère.)
" When one has no mother, one must be suckled by one's grandmother."— [*Louisiana.*]

269. Quand ou tini malhé sépent mò.é ou pa lakhè. (Quand vous êtes dans le malheur le serpent vous mord par la queue.)
" When you're in ill-luck, a snake can bite you even with its tail."—[*Martinique.*]

270. Quand ou mangé evec guiabe, quimbé cuillè ou longue. (Quand vous mangez avec le diable, tenez votre cuillère longue.)
" When you eat with the devil, see that your spoon is long."—[*Martinique.*]

271. * Quand patate tchuite, faut mangé li. (Quand la patate est cuite, il faut la manger.)
" When the sweet potato is cooked, it must be eaten."4—[*Louisiana.*]

272. Quand poul ou tini zé, pas mette li dans canari. (Quand votre poule pond des œufs, ne la mettez pas dans le pot.)
" When your hen is laying, don't put her in the pot."5—[*Martinique.*]

---

1 It is needless to undertake what we have not ability to carry out.
2 Said to those who talk hopefully of impossibilities.
3 Refers to obstinacy. A man may be compelled to move his feet, but not to change his resolve.
4 This differs a little from the spelling adopted by Gottschalk in his *Bamboula*—" *Quand patate-la couite ma va mangé li.*" The proverb is used in the sense of our saying : " Strike the iron while it's hot."
5 Like our saying about killing the goose that laid the golden eggs.

273. Quand prend trop boucoup, li glissé. (Quand on prend trop [lit.: "trop beaucoup"], cela glisse.
    "Grab for too much, and it slips away from you."—[*Mauritius.*]

274. Quand vente crié zoréyes sourde. (Quand le ventre crie, les oreilles sont sourdes.)
    "When the belly cries, the ears are deaf."—[*Mauritius.*]

275. Quand vente faim, siprit vini. (Quand le ventre a faim, l'esprit vient.)
    "An empty stomach brings wit;"—lit.: When the stomach is empty, wit comes."¹
    —[*Mauritius.*]

276. Quand vous guétte làhaut vous liziés vine pitit. (Quand vous regardez en haut, vos yeux rapetissent.)
    "When you look overhead, your eyes become small."—[*Mauritius.*]

277. Quand yo baille ou tête bef pou mangé, n'a pas peur zieux li. (Quand on vous donne une tête de bœuf à manger n'ayez pas peur de ses yeux.)
    "When you are given an ox's head to eat, don't be afraid of his eyes."—[*Hayti*]

278. Quiquefois wou plante zharicots rouze ; zharicots blancs qui poussé. (Quelquefois vous plantez des haricots rouges, et ce sont des haricots blancs qui poussent.)
    "Sometimes you sow red beans, and white beans grow." "The best-laid plans of mice and men gang aft a-gley."—[*Mauritius.*]

279. Quand yon bâtiment cassé ça pas empêché les zautt navigué. (Quand un bâtiment est cassé, ça n'empêche pas les autres de naviguer.)
    "When a ship is broken (*wrecked*), the accident does not prevent others from sailing."²
    —[*Martinique.*]

280. Qui mê'é zefs nans calenda oûoches? (Qui a mêlé (mis) des œufs dans la calinda des roches [pierres.]?)
    "What business have eggs in the calinda—*i. e.* dance—of stones?" (*Calinda,* said to be derived from the Spanish *que linda!*—"how beautiful!")³—[*Trinidad.*]

281. Rann sévice baïll mal dos. (Rendre service donne mal au dos.)
    "Doing favors gives one the back-ache."—[*Martinique.*]

282. *Ratte mangé canne, zanzoli mouri innocent. (Le rat mange la canne-[à-sucre], le lézard en meurt.)
    "'Tis the rat eats the cane ; but the lizard dies for it."⁴—[*Louisiana.*]

283. Ravett pas janmain asséz fou pou li allé lapòte pouleillé. (Le ravet n'est jamais assez fou pour aller à la porte du poulailler)
    "The cockroach is never silly enough to approach the door of the hen-house."—[*Martinique.*]

---

¹ *Wit*, that is, "mother-wit"—common-sense.
² There is a Portuguese proverb to the same effect: "Shipwrecks have never deterred navigation."
³ The author of *Les Bambous* mentions the *bèlè, caleinda, quiouba* and *biguine*, slave-dances of Martinique. *Dansé yon caleinda marré* (to dance the *calinda* or *caleinda* tied up) meant to receive a whipping.
⁴ This proverb is certainly of West Indian origin, though I first obtained it from a Louisianian. In consequence of the depredations committed by rats in the West-Indian cane-fields, it is customary after the crop has been taken off, to fire the dry cane tops and leaves. The blaze, spreading over the fields, destroys many rats, but also a variety of harmless lizards and other creatures.

284. *Ravette pas jamain tini raison douvant poule. (Le ravet n'a jamais raison devant la poule.)
"Cockroach is never in the right where the fowl is concerned"—(lit.. *befor(the fowl.)*[1]
—[*Trinidad.*]

285. Rasiers tini zorcïes. (Les [rosiers?] buissons ont des oreilles.)
"Bushes have ears."—[*Trinidad.*]

286. *Rendé service, baille chagrin. (Rendre service donne du chagrin.)
"Doing favors brings sorrow."—[*Louisiana.*]

287. Roce entété. més quand téti cause av li, li répondé. (La roche est entôtée, mais quand le têtu lui parle, elle répond.)
"The rock's hard-headed; but when the stone-hammer speaks to him, he answers"
—[*Títu* means an obstinate person, also a stone-hammer.] 2 - '.*Mauritius.*]

288. Sac vide pas ka tienne douboutt. (Un sac vide ne peut pas se tenir debout.)
"An empty sack cannot stand up." One cannot work with an empty stomach.- -
[*Martinique.*]

289. Sèpent dit li pas rhaï mounn-la qui cué li; c'est ça qui dit, "Mi sèpent!" (Le serpent dit qu'il ne hait pas la personne qui le tue; que c'est celle qui dit, "Voilà le serpent!")
"The snake says he doesn't hate the person who kills him, but the one who calls out, 'Look at the snake!'"—[*Martinique.*]

290. Serin dérobé; maille bengali. (Le serin se derobe; prenez lo bengali.)
"When the canary can't be found, take the bengalee." When you can't find what you like, be content with what you can get."—[*Mauritius.*]

291. Si coulev oûlé viv, li pas prouminéo grand-chimin. (Si la couleuvre veut vivre, elle ne se promène pas dans le grand chemin).
"If the snake cares to live, it doesn't journey upon the high-road."—[*Guyana.*]

292. Si coulève pas té fonté,[3] femmes só pouend li fair ribans jipes. (Si la couleuvre n'était pas effrontée, les femmes la prendraient pour en faire des rubans de jupes).
"If the snake wasn't spunky, women would use it for petticoat string."— *Trinidad.*]

293. Si crapaud die ous caïman tini mal ziex, coèr-li. (Si le crapaud vous dit que le caïman a mal aux yeux, croyez-le).
"If the frog tells you the alligator has sore eyes, believe him!" 4—[*Trinidad.*]

294. Si jipon ou k'allé bien, pas chaché mette kilott nhomme ou. (Si votre jupon vous va bien, ne cherchez pas à mettre la culotte de votre mari.)
"If your petticoat fits you well, don't try to put on your husband's breeches."—
[*Martinique.*]

1 I find this proverb in every dialect I have been able to study. In Martinique Creole the words vary slightly: "*Douvant poule ravett pas ni raison.*"
2 This is another example of double-punning, of which we have already had a specimen in Prov 163.
3 *Fonté* (for *effronté*) has quite an extensive meaning in Creole. It may refer to the impudence of a badly brought-up child, or to the over-familiarity on the part of an adult; but it may also refer to high spirit, pluck, independence of manner. A colored mother once told me I should be surprised to see how *fonté* her son had become since he had been going to school. She meant, of course, that the lad was growing "smart," active, plucky.
4 Similarity of habits and of experience is necessary to guarantee the trustworthiness of testimony regarding those we do not know.

295. * Si lamèr té bouilli, poissons sré tchuite. (Si la mer bouillait, les poissons seraient cuits).
" If the sea were to boil, the fishes would be cooked."—[*Louisiana*.]

296. Si lasavane té ka palé nous sé connaitt trop désigret. (Si la savanne parlait, nous connaîtrions trop de secrets).
"If the fields could talk, we should know too many secrets." 1 —[*Martinique*.]

297. Si léphant pas té savé boyaux li gouous, li pas sé valé calebasses. (Si l'élephant n'avait pas su qu'il avait de gros boyaux, il n'aurait pas avalé des calébasses).
" If the elephant didn't know that he had big guts, he wouldn't have swallowed calabashcs."—[*Trinidad*.]

298. * "Si-moin-tè-connaitt pas janmain douvant; li toujou derè. (Si-je-l'avais-su n'est jamais devant; il vient toujours derrière.) ∖
'' If-I-had-only-known ' is never before one ; he always comes behind."—[*Martinique*.

299. Si moin té gagnin moussa, moin té mangé gombo. (Si j'avais du moussa, je mangerais du gombo).
" If I had some *moussa* 2 I would eat some gombo." If I had the necessary I could enjoy the superfluous."—[*Martinique*.]

300. Si té pas gagné soupé nens moune, moune ka touffé. (S'il n'y avait pas de soupirs dans le monde, le monde étoufferait).
"If there were no sighing in the world, the world would stifle."3 —[Quoted by Alphonse Daudet.]

301. Si zannoli té bon viann, li sè pas ka drivé lassous baïe. (Si le lézard était bon à manger [lit.: bonne viande], il ne se trouverait point sous une baille.)
" If the lizard were good to eat, it would never be found under a tub."4—[*Martinique*.]

302. Soleil couché ; malbèr pas jamain couché. (Le soleil se couche ; le malheur ne se couche jamais.)
"The sun sets; misfortune never sets."—[*Hayti*.]

303. * Soleil levé là; li couché là. (Le soleil se lève là ; il se couche là.)
"Sun rises there [pointing to the east] ; he sets there" [pointing to the west]5— [*Louisiana*.]

304. Souliers faraud, més domage ziutes manze lipieds. (Les souliers sont elegants, mais c'est dommage qu'ils mangent les pieds.)
" Shoes are fine things; but it's a pity they bite one's feet."6—'*Mauritius*]

---

1 " If walls had ears," etc.
2 *Mousse* is a word used in *Martinique* for hominy, or a sort of corn-mush which is used to thicken gombo-soup. In Louisiana boiled rice is similarly used.
3 I found this proverb cite ł in Daudet's article on Tourguèneff in the November *Century* [1883]. The accentuation was incorrect. *Moun, or moune,* Creole form of French *monde*, is generally used to signify people in general—*folks*—not the world.
4 Thomas gives us a briefer Trinidad version : *Si zandoli té bon viâne, le pas sé ka drivé* (il ne se trouverait pas) : "If a lizard were good meat, it wouldn't easily be found."
5 A proverb common to all the dialects. In uttering it, with emphatic gesture, the negro signifies that there is no pride which will not be at last brought down, no grandeur which will not have an end.
6 M. Baissac tells us, in a very amusing way, how this proverb originated at the time of the negro emancipation in Mauritius, when 30.000 pairs of new shoes were distributed. Another saying, equally characteristic, was—" *Lhère li entré dans vous lacase, souliers dans lipieds ; lhère li dans grand cimin, souliers dans mouçoirs* " :—(When he enters your house, his shoes are on his feet; but once he is on the public road, they are in his handkerchief.)

305. * Tafia toujou dîe la vérité. (Le tafia dit toujours la vérité.
"Tafia always tells the truth."1—[*Louisiana*.]

306. Tambou tini grand train pace endidans li vide. (Le tambour va [lit : tient] grand train parcequ'il est vide en dedans.)
"The drum makes a great fuss because it is empty inside."2—[*Trinidad*.]

307. Tampée ka gagnen malhèrs ka doublons pas sa gueri. (Un 'tampée' achète des malheurs que les doublons ne peuvent pas guerir.)
"A penny buys troubles that doubloons cannot cure."—[*Trinidad*.]

308. * "Tant-pis" n'a pas cabane. ("Tant-pis" n'a pas de cabane.)
"'So-much-the-worse" has no cabin.'"3—[*Louisiana*.]

309. Temps moune connaîte l'aûte nans grand jou, nans nouîte yeaux pas besoàn chandelle pou clairér yeaux. (Quand on connait quelqu'un [lit : un autre] dans le grand jour, dans la nuit on n'a pas besoin d'une chandelle pour s'éclairer.)
"When one person knows another by broad daylight, he doesn't need a candle to recognize him at night."4—[*Trinidad*.]

310. * Temps present gagnin assez comme ça avec so quenne. (Le temps present en a assez comme ça avec le sien.)
"The present has enough to do to mind its own affairs."5—[*Louisiana*]

311. * Ti chien, ti côdon. (Petit chien, petit lien.)
"A little string for a little dog."—[*Martinique.*]

312. Ti hache coupé gouaus bois. (Une petite hache coupe un grand arbre.)
"A little axe cuts down a big tree."—[*Martinique.*]

313. Ti moun cònnaitt couri, yo pas cònnaitt serré. (Les enfants—lit : "le petit monde"—savent courir ; ils ne savent pas se cacher.)
"Children (little folk) know how to run; they do not know how to hide."—[*Martinique*.]

314. Tig mô, chien ka prend pays. (Quand le tigre est mort, le chien prend le pays.)
"When the tiger is dead, the dog takes [rules] the country."—[*Martinique*.]

315. Tòtì sé vole si li tè tini plimm. (Le tortue volerait si elle avait des ailes.)
"The tortoise would fly it it had wings."6—[*Martinique.*]

---

1 *Tafia* is the rum extracted from sugar-cane. "*In vino veritas.*"

2 In Louisiana Creole, *faire di-train* is commonly used in the sense of making a great noise, a big fuss. An old negro-servant might often be heard reproving the children of the house in some such fashion as this:—" *Ga!—pouki tapé fait tou di-train la ?—Toulé pé ?—pas fait tou di-train mo di toi!*" (Here, what are you making all that noise for?—are you going to keep quiet?—musn't make so much noise, I tell you !")

3 This proverb is the retort for the phrase: "So much the worse for you." Sometimes one might hear a colored servant for example, warning the children of the house to keep out of the kitchen, which in Creole residences usually opens into the great court-yard where the little ones play: *Eh, pitis ! faut pas resté là : vous ka casser tout!* ("Hey ! little ones, musn't stay there; you'll break everything!") If the father or mother should then exclaim "*Tant pis pour eux !*"—so much the worse for them if they do break everything, you would hear the old woman reply: "*Tant-pis n'a pas cabane!*"—"So-much-the-worse has no cabin"—i. e., nothing to lose. She believes in an ounce of prevention rather than a pound of cure.

4 When a person has once given us positive evidence of his true character, we do not need any information as to what that person will do under certain circumstances.

5 Literally the proverb is almost untranslateable. It is cited to those who express needless apprehension of future misfortune. "*Mo va gagnin malhé*"—(I am going to have trouble.) "*Aïe, alé! chère!—temps present gagnin assez comme ça avec so quenne.*" (Ah, my dear ! the present has enough trouble of its own.)

6 "Pigs might fly," etc.

316. Tout bois cé bois:
    Main mapou
    Pas 'cajou.
    (Tout bois c'est du bois;
    Mais le mapou
    N'est pas de l'acajou.)
    "All wood is wood; but mapou wood isn't mahogany (cedar) "[1]—[*Trinidad.*]

317 * Tout ça c'est commerce Man Lison. (Tout ça c'est affaire de Maman Lison.)
    "All that's like Mammy Lison's doings."[2]—[*Louisiana.*]

318. Tout ça qui poté zépron pas maquignon. (Tout homme qui porte éperons n'est pas
    maquignon.)
    "Everybody who wears spurs isn't a jockey." All is not gold that glitters.—
    [*Martinique.*]

319. Toutt cabinett tini maringouin. (Tout cabinet contient des maringouins.)
    "Every bed-chamber has its mosquitoes in it."—Equivalent to our own proverb: A
    skeleton in every closet.—|*Martinique.*]

320.—* Toutt joué c'est joué; mais cassé bois dans bonda macaque—ça pas joué. (Tout
    [façon de] jouer c'est jouer; mais ce n'est pas jouer que de casser du bois dans le
    derrière du macaque.)
    . . . . [3]—[*Martinique.*]

321. *,Toutt jour c'est pas dimanche. (Tous les jours ne sont pas le dimanche.)
    "Every day isn't Sunday."—*Louisiana.*

322. Tou jwé sa jwé; me bwa là zòrè sa pa jwó. (Tout [façon de] jouer c'est jouer; mais
    enfoncer du bois dans l'oreille n'est pa3 jouer.)
    "All play is play; but poking a piece of wood into one's ear isn't play."—[*Guyane.*]

323. *Tout macaque trouvé so piti joli. (Tout macaque trouve son petit joli.)
    "Every monkey thinks its young one pretty."—[*Louisiana*]

324. Toutt milett ni grand zaureilles. (Tout les mulets ont des grandes oreilles.)
    "All mules have big ears."—Equivalent to our proverb: "Birds of a feather flock
    together."—*Martinique.*

---

1 Thomas translates c'you by "cedar." *Acajou* in French, signifies mahogany, as it does
also in Louisiana Creole. There is an old song, of which the refrain is:
    Chèr bijou
    D'acajou,
    Mo laimin vous
    ("My darling mahogany jewel, I love you!")

2 Whenever a thing is badly done, this saying is used:—*commerce* in the Creole
signifying almost the reverse of what it does in French. Who that traditional *Man Lison*
was, I have never been able to find out.

3 This ridiculous observation is unsuitable for translation. Nevertheless we have an
English, or perhaps an American, proverb equally vulgar, which may have inspired, or been
derived from, the Creole one. In the English saying, the words "joking" and "provoking"
are used as rhymes. The moral is precisely similar to that of No. 322.
    In old days the Creole story-teller would always announce his intention of beginning
a tale by the exclamation "*Tim-tim!*" whereupon the audience would shout in reply,
"*Bois sec;*" and the story-teller would cry again, "*Cassez-li,*" to which the chorus would add
".... *dans tchu* (bonda) *macaque.*" Thus the story-teller intimated that he had no inten-
tion of merely "*joking,*" but intended to tell the whole truth and nothing else—"a real good
story"—*tois fois bonne conte!*

325.—*Toutt mounn save ça qui ka bouï nens canari yo. (Toute personne sait ce qui bout dans son canari [marmite].)

"Everybody knows what boils in his own pot"—i. e., knows his own business best.[1]—[*Martinique.*]

326. Travaï pas mal; cé ziex qui capons. [(Le travail ne fait pas du mal; c'est les yeux qui sont capons [lâches].)

" Work doesn't hurt ;—'tis the eyes that are cowards."—[*Mauritius.*]

327. Trop gratté bourlé. (Trop gratter brûle [cuit].)

" Too much scratching brings smarting."—[*Mauritius.*]

328. Trop profi crévé poche. (Trop de profit crève la poche.)

"Too much profit bursts one's pockets."--[*Martinique.*]

329. Tropp bijou, gâde-mangé vide. (Trop de bijoux, garde-manger vide.)

"Too much jewelry, empty cupboard."—[*Martinique.*]

330. Vente enflé, mouces zaune té pique li. (Le ventre enflé, les mouches jaunes l'ont piqué.)[2]
. . . . —[*Mauritius*]

331. Vide éne boutéye pour rempli laute, qui li? (Vider une bouteille pour en remplir une autre, qu'est-ce ?)

" What's the good of emptying one bottle only to fill another ?"[3]—[*Mauritius.*]

332. * Vie cannari ka fé bon bouillon. (Les vieux pots font les bonnes soupes.)

" It's the old pot that makes the good soup."—[*Martinique.*]

333. Vié cœq, zône poule. (Vieux coq, jeune poule.)

" An old cock, a young hen."—[*Mauritius.*]

334. Volè pas ainmein voué canmarade yo pòté sac. (Les voleurs n'aiment pas voir leurs camarades portant le sacs.)

" Thieves do not like to see their comrades carrying the bags."[4]—[*Martinique.*]

335. Vous napas va montré vié zaco fère grimaces. (Vous ne montrerez pas à un vieux singe à faire des grimaces.)

" You can't teach an old monkey how to make faces."[5]—[*Mauritius.*]

336. Voyé chein, chein voyé lakhe li. (Envoyez le chien, et le chien envoie sa queue.)

"Send dog, and dog sends his tail."—Refers to those who obey orders only by proxy.—[*Trinidad*]

---

[1] In Thomas's Trinidad version: " *Tout moune connaite ça qui ka bou[î] nans canari yeaux*." In Louisiana Creole: " *Chakin connin ça kap' bouilli dans so chodùere.*" *Canari* is sometim s used in our Creole, but rarely. I have only heard it in old songs. The iron pot (*chodière*) or tin utensil has superseded the *canari*

[2] This proverb is scarcely suitable for English translation; but the forcible and picturesque irony of it will be appreciated in M. Baissac's explanatory note: " *Comment se l'expliquer autrement en dehors du mariage.*"

[3] Same signification as Prov. 138.

[4] Probably truer to human nature than our questionable statement concerning " honor among thieves." Mr. Bigelow, in his contribution to *Harper's Magazine*, cited a similar proverb in the Haytian dialect.

[5] "Teach your granny to suck eggs."

337. Yo ka quimbé¹ chritiens pa langue yo, bef pa còne yo. (On prend les Chrétiens par la langue, les bœufs par les cornes.)
"Christians are known by their tongues, oxen by their horns." (Literally, are taken by or caught by.)—[*Martinique.*]

338. Yon doègt pas sa pouend pice. (Un seul doigt ne peut pas attraper des puces.)
"One finger can't catch fleas."—[*Martinique.*]

339. * Yon lanmain douè lavé laute. (Une main doit laver l'autre.)
"One hand must wash the other."—You must not depend upon others to get you out of trouble.—[*Martinique.*]

340. Yon mauvais paòle ka blessé plis qu'coupd'roche. (Une mauvaise parole blesse plus qu'un coup-de-pierre.)
"A wicked word hurts more than a blow from a stone."—[*Martinique.*]

341. Zaco malin, li-méme té montré noir coment voler. (La singe est malin; c'est lui qui a montré au noir comment on vole.)
"The monkey is sly; it was he that first taught the black man how to steal."—[*Mauritius.*]

---

¹ *Quimbé* is a verb of African origin. It survives in Louisiana Creole as *tchombé* or *chombo* :

    Caroline, zolie femme.
    Chombo moin dans collet.

["Caroline, pretty woman; put your arm about my neck!"—lit.: "take me by the neck."]

There are other African words used by the older colored women, such as *macayé*, meaning to eat at all hours; and *Ouendé*, of which the sense is dubious. But the Congo verb *fifa*, to kiss; and the verbs *souyé*, to flatter ; *pougalé*, to abuse violently; and such nouns as *saff* (glutton), *yche* or *iche* (baby), which are preserved in other Creole dialects, are apparently unknown in Louisiana to-day.

In Chas. Jeannest's work, *Quatre Années au Congo* [Paris: Charpentier, 1883], I find a scanty vocabulary of words in the Fiot dialect, the native dialect of many slaves imported into Louisiana and the West Indies. In this vocabulary the word *ouenda* is translated by "partir pour." I fancy it also signifies " to be absent, and that it is synonymous with our Louisiana African-Creole *ouendé*, preserved in the song :

    Ouendé, ou-ndé, macaya ;
    Mo pas, 'barassé, macaya !
    Ouendé, ouendé, macaya ;
    Mo bois bon divin, macaya!
    Ouendé, ouen té, macaya;
    Mo mangé bon poulé, macaya!
    Ouendé, ouendé, macaya;.. etc.

This is one of the very few songs with a purely African refrain still sung in New Orleans. The theme seems to be that, the master and mistress of a house being absent, some slave is encouraging a slave-friend to eat excessively. to "stuff himself" with wine, chicken, etc. "They are gone, friend : eat, fill yourself; *I'm* not a bit ashamed; stuff yourself !— I'm drinking good wine; stuff yourself !—I'm eating good chicken ; gorge yourself," etc. Here *ouendé* seems to mean "they are out; they are gone away,"—therefore there is no danger.

There is another Creole song with the same kind of double refrain, but the meaning of the African words I have not been able to discover.

    Nicolas, Nicolas, Nicolas, ou dindin ;'
    Nicolas, Nicolas, Nicolas marché ouaminon:
        Quand li marché
          Ouarasi. ouarasa !
        Quand li marché
          Ouarasi, ouarava!

[" Nicholas, etc., you are a turkey-cock! Nicholas walks *ouaminon:* when he walks, it is *ouarsi, ouarasa.*"] The idea is obvious enough; viz.: that Nicholas struts like a turkey-cock ; but the precise signification of the three italicised words I have failed to learn.

342. Zaco napas guétte so laquée; li guétte pour son camarade. (Le singe ne regarde pas sa queue ; il regarde celle de son voisin.)
"Monkey never watches his own tail; he watches his neighbor's."—[*Mauritius.*]

343. *Zaffaire ça qui sotte, chien mangé diné yo. (Des choses [qui appartiennent] aux sots les chiens font leur dîner.)
"Dogs make their dinner upon what belongs to fools."—[*Louisiana.*]

344. *Z ffé cabritt pa zaffé mouton. (L'affaire de la chèvre n'est pas l'affaire du mouton.)
"The goat's business is not the sheep's affair." [1]—[*Martinique.*]

345. Zaffóre qui fine passé narien; laute qui pour vini qui li! (L'affaire passée n'est rien ; c'est l'affaire à venir qui est le hic.)
"What's past is nothing; it's what's to come that's the rub."—[*Mauritius.*]

346. Zamais béf senti so corne trop lourd. (Jamais le bœuf ne sent ses cornes trop lourdes.)
"The ox never finds his horns too heavy to carry."—[*Mauritius.*]

347. Zamés disel dire li salé. (Le sel ne dit jamais qu'il est salé.)
"The salt never says that it is salty." True virtue never boasts.—[*Mauritius.*]

348. Zaureille pas tini couv éti. (Les oreilles n'ont pas de couverture.)
"There is no covering for the ears."—[*Martinique.*]

349. Zié beké brilé zié nèg. (Les yeux du blanc brûle les yeux du nègre.)
"The white man's eyes burn the negro's eyes." [2]—[*Martinique.*]

350. Zié rouge pas boulé savann. (Les yeux rouges ne brûlent pas la savane.)
"Red eyes can't burn the savannah." A better translation might be: "Red eyes can't start a prairie-fire." The meaning, is that mere anger avails nothing. [3]—[*Martinique.*]

351. Zouré napas ena lentérement. (Les jurons n'ont pas d'enterrement.)
"Curses don't make funerals."—[*Mauritius.*]

352. Zozo paillenqui crié là-haut, coudevent vini. (Le paille-en-cul crie la-haut, le coup de vent vient.)
"When the tropic-bird screams overhead, a storm-wind is coming."—[*Mauritius.*]

---

[1] Seems to be the same in all Creole dialects, excepting that the rabbit is sometimes substituted for the sheep.

[2] *Béké* is translated by *blanc* in Turiault's work ; but the witty author of *Les Bambous* writes: *Nèg* se dit pour *esclave*, et *béké* pour *maître*. Therefore perhaps a more correct translation would be: "The master's eyes burn the slave's eyes." The phrase recalls a curious refrain which used to be sung by Louisiana field-hands:

Tout, tout. pays blanc—Danié qui commandé,
Danié qui commandé ça !
Danié qui commandé.

["All, all the country white" (white-man's country); "Daniel has so commanded," etc. I do not know whether the prophet Daniel is referred to.

[3] In the Guyane patois, they say : "*Ça qui gadé gran boi yé kôlé pa brûlé yé.*" (*Celui qui regarde les grands bois avec des yeux colères ne les brûle pas.*)

INDEX TO VARIOUS DIALECTS.

INDEX TO SUBJECTS OF PROVERBS.

LA CUISINE CREOLE.

A compilation of many original Creole and other valuable recipes obtained from noted Southern housewives, with a number of *chefs d'œuvre* from leading *chefs*, who have made New Orleans famous for its cuisine.

Published by WILL H. COLEMAN,

70 ASTOR HOUSE, NEW YORK.